Thi

A Short & Straightforward History of the Third Reich

(The History and Legacy of Nazi Germany under Adolf Hitler)

Walter Davis

Published By **Matt Hall**

Walter Davis

Third Reich: A Short & Straightforward History of the Third Reich (The History and Legacy of Nazi Germany under Adolf Hitler)

ISBN 978-1-998769-22-3

Legal & Disclaimer

The information contained in this ebook is not designed to replace or take the place of any form of medicine or professional medical advice. The information in this ebook has been provided for educational & entertainment purposes only.

The information contained in this book has been compiled from sources deemed reliable, and it is accurate to the best of the Author's knowledge; however, the Author cannot guarantee its accuracy and validity and cannot be held liable for any errors or omissions. Changes are periodically made to this book. You must consult your doctor or get professional medical advice before using any of the suggested remedies, techniques, or information in this book.

Upon using the information contained in this book, you agree to hold harmless the Author from and against any damages, costs, and expenses, including any legal fees potentially resulting from the application of any of the information provided by this guide. This disclaimer applies to any damages or injury caused by the use and application, whether directly or indirectly, of any advice or information presented, whether for breach of contract, tort, negligence, personal injury, criminal intent, or under any other cause of action.

You agree to accept all risks of using the information presented inside this book. You need to consult a professional medical practitioner in order to ensure you are both able and healthy enough to participate in this program.

Table Of Contents

Chapter 1: How Did The Events Factors Influenced The Events............................ 1

Chapter 2: What Was The Motivation Behind Adolf Hitler?............................... 27

Chapter 3: The Early Stages Of Being 47

Chapter 4: Commerce And Commerce... 82

Chapter 5: The Jewish Question........... 114

Chapter 6: Second World War 137

Chapter 7: The Treasure 167

Chapter 8: Was Hitler Mad?................. 182

Chapter 1: How Did The Events Factors Influenced The Events

It was in the early year 1933 that the tensions in Berlin increased, announcing that the country of Weimar was over. nation of Weimar. Twenty-eight days into the new Year on January 28 the General Kurt Von Schleicher - the state's chancellor - after 57 days in the office was dismissed by General Marshal Von Hindenburg. The tragic winter weekend will be recorded in History to determine the fate of Germany for a century to follow.

Adolf Hitler, the chairman of the Nationalist Socialist Party, had been a fervent believer for two years prior to made his offer for election as chancellor. However, he was repeatedly rejected. Although the Weimar republic from its beginning was a huge success, it was nearly thirteen years on, in the month of the new year there were discussions about Putsch (German to mean Coup) in the hands of one political party as well as its many generals.

Adolf Hitler had always dreamed of uniting Germany and Austria with the German Flag. All his efforts were aimed at ensuring that. Did anyone know that this thought that was conceived in the mind of a madman became the solemn pledge to conquer the entire nation of Germany?

The Dr. Joseph Goebbels, as was praised by David Irving in this book as the genius behind the Third Reich, in his biography in the book, wrote that Monday June 30 was a solemn and solemn day for the people of Germany. Hitler was their leader. was in the chancellery to decide the future of the country; with others Nazi generals, Goebbels was seated in front of at the gate of Kaiserhof in anticipation of the expression of their leader. They believed that they it would be possible to determine the difference between winning or not, from his face. He was certain they'd be able to discern his facesince they had been standing outside of these gates, but rarely for a couple of years. it was like a feeling of déjà vu, to anticipate failure or joy, or just awe was they ever successful.

They only wanted an amazing experience And they were in the middle of it, witnessing it for themselves.

What did you think was Adolf Hitler? A sickly child born in the town of no importance of Braunau-on the-Inn. The town itself was split in half separated by Austria and Germany and Germany, a union that was the goal of nearly all children born in the region, or at most likely to dedicate their entire life to the cause of like he did when he was the lowest-class person nobody was aware of in Vienna.

Before we get into the details of the events that took place, it's important to first understand how he got to where he is today after the Third Reich series of events.

The Nazi Party developed into a massive development, and was able to control Germany by using extremist tactics between 1933 and 1945 under the direction from Adolf Hitler (1889-1945). In 1919, it was established as an organization known as the German Workers' Party the group promoted German pride, and was opposed to Semitism and expressed displeasure with and displeasure with the Treaty of Versailles' details. The 1919 peace agreement ended World War I (1914-1918) and was expected to force Germany to accept several concessions and compensations. Hitler joined the group at the time it was formed and became its leader in 1921. In 1933, Hitler was elected chancellor of Germany and his administration quickly became a tyrant. the hands of tyrannical forces. Following the devastation of Germany during World War II (1939-45) and the Nazi Party saw its most desired ending. A lot of

Of its top officials were sentenced to life imprisonment for crimes associated with the murder of around 6 millions European Jews during the Holocaust.

Nazi Party Origins

In 1919, veteran of the armed forces Adolf Hitler, baffled by the German defeat in World War I, left the nation. He was financially stricken and uncertain in his political outlook, but he enrolled in an association of political leaders known as"The German Workers' Part. It was founded in the same year by a small group of men that included the locksmith Anton Drexler (1884-1942) and writer Karl Harrer (1890-1926), the group promoted German patriotic values and opposed Semitism. The underlying idea was they believed that it was the Treaty of Versailles, the harmony agreement that ended this war was damaging to Germany in that it required reparations that the country could never afford. In the ensuing years, Hitler tapped into being an enthralling public speaker and began to attract new members by the need to accuse Jews as well as Marxists of German issues, and even embracing a flamboyant patriotism with the notion of the Aryan "ace race."

On July 19, 1921, the German leader formally accepted the authority of the group, then renamed"the Nationalist Socialist German Workers' (Nazi) Party.

The whole time, his rule was bloody and brutal. But, perhaps more horrific were the events that brought him to his appointment as the new Fuehrer.

It was the latter half of the 18th century, following the time that the United States had announced its independence from Great Britain. Central Europe was then an grouping of around 300 states.

In the beginning of the nineteenth century Germany included 39 states which all shared a few common political goals. In the year of the German Confederation's name, in 1815 the states merged to join the economies of all states that spoke German. There are those people who believe that had this concept been a success Germany today would have grown and held more power over the globe than it currently does However, in the moment of its creation it was a time when the German Confederation was a stout opponent to all that a true German Nationalist would stand for.

Before it could be proved, it fell in a matter of years because of the increasing tensions between the two nations that were Austria as well as Prussia. There were many talks, but they fell out and a seven-year war following, Germany came to be called the German Empire or, more precisely the beginning of what was to become the initial German Reich which was headed by the chancellor of the first time, Otto Von Bismarck.

Many ways Adolf Hitler and Otto Bismarck are one in the same. However, the two nationalists who are both in the same boat would never get to meet. The first was only nine an old at the time that other passed away. However many among them, including Adolf's close family members believed that he in a twisted manner admiring the vision Bismarck set for an unification of Germany however Bismarck failed to bring Austria under the German flag.

First Reich (Germany's unification) been able to bring every one of the German countries under the flag of Germany, with the exception of Austria. There are numerous theories as to what caused it as well. Adolf Hitler, in his own view, viewed the event as

A plan to ignore Austria and Germany, as his greatest weakness was his affection for Austria as well as Germany together.

It was a well-known reality it was known that Austria and Prussia did not have a love affair with each other. When the negotiations for Unified Germany began, Austria itself was not keen to be a part of it. Austria was a monarchy with a dual system and would have to sacrifice to be part of the unification of Germany which was an Prussia dominant Germany and this is why King Habsburg, the ruler of the Holy Roman Empire, neglected the issue.

Otto Von Bismarck led the first German Reich in 1871 by the exclusion of Austria.

However, this also resulted in the rise of German nationalist sentiment, which was later led by numerous powerful dictators and leaders, and that has consumed the German population.

Otto Von Bismarck was an expert in the field of military and politics. He ruled the newly created German Empire with a strong grasp. Similar to Hitler He was a clever man and skilled at manipulating people according to his own will. Most importantly, what they shared was their love of Germany. A united nation that was thriving, and according to their dreams, was ruled over the whole of Europe. He was the most influential Prussian politician Germany has seen throughout its history.

Paul Von Hindenburg and Erich Ludendorff were the leaders of the unification of Germany throughout World War I, which was a challenging job because they did not have similar goals or the capacity to control the control of the reins. They did their best to guide the nation through the chaos of the War that was the first of its kind. The same month in November brought about another revolution that ended monarchy in all of Europe and bringing about Nazism as a notion and power that was given to one of the soldiers who had been a soldier and survived the battle in Vienna and was named Adolf Hitler.

The foundation that is Nazi Germany will remain its Weimar Republic, or later according to Hitler's words be referred to in the Second Reich. Germany went from a federation that was run by the royal family and a monarch to a democratic system until the Nazi rebellion in 1933 marked the end of.

The Weimar Republic was Germany's legislature between 1919 and 1933, which was the time period following World War I until Hitler's rule began. The constitution was created by a meeting of the people following Kaiser Wilhelm II's surrender.

From uncertain beginnings to a brief period achievement and an euphoria of immense sadness The Weimar Republic experienced turmoil to position Germany in the ascendancy to the rise of Adolf Hitler and the Nazi Party.

The Weimar Constitution was signed into law by President Ebert on August 11 1919. The law was met with venomous opposition from the military as well as the extreme left. The constitution had 181 articles that protected everything in to the German State (Reich) as well as the German citizens' rights to a strict standard of opportunity, and also the way in which laws must be interpreted.

It was the Weimar Constitution incorporated these features:

A Reich Minister or the Chancellor Reich Minister must be in support of the President in all actions.

* Article 48 allows presidents to suspend his social liberties and to work without restriction in the event of a crisis.

* Two governing bodies (the Reichstag and the Reichsrat) were to represent those who were the German public.

* All Germans enjoy similar rights and responsibilities.

* All Germans have the right to articulate.

* All Germans have the right to have a peaceful gathering.

* All Germans have the right to having the option of religion; there isn't a state-run church.

* Government-funded, state-run instruction is free and obligatory for kids.

* All Germans are entitled to private property.

* All Germans have the right to pursue opportunities and earning within the workplace.

Inflation, Hyperinflation as well as the Fallout

No matter the new constitution however, regardless of its new constitution, the Weimar Republic confronted one of the most prominent financial challenges facing Germany that was hyperinflation. Due to the Treaty of Versailles, Germany's capacity to provide income-generating iron and coal mineral decreased. In the wake of war and reparations, which reduced its budget as reparations and war obligations drained its funds, the German government was unable to pay its debts.

A section of the World War I Allies did not agree with Germany's claim that it couldn't afford to pay. In an unobtrusive League of Nations penetrate, French and Belgian soldiers in Germany's most important industrial zone, called the Ruhr Valley, resolved to receive their installments of reparation.

The Weimar government urged German specialists to be active in opposing the occupation, and even picket shutting down coal mine shafts as well as iron processing plants. So, the German economy instantly was ruined.

So the Weimar government basically printed more money. The effort exploded backwards and further degraded German mark. Inflation grew to an alarming rate. The price of basic products soared rapidly and many people lost everything they owned.

In the period of hyperinflation those in the German working class was enduring the most severe part of the financial chaos. After a short time they were exhausted and skeptical regarding their government. In search of a fresh idea and fearing the possibility of a Communist invasion, a lot of people went to gatherings with radical ideas like those of the Nazi Party led by Adolf Hitler despite his displeasing and bombed attempt to start an uprising in the streets in 1923.

In 1932 in 1932, The Nazi Party turned into the largest party in the Parliament. After a brief struggle to gain the power of the party, Hitler was named Chancellor in January 1933. Within a short time he resorted to Article 48 of the Weimar Constitution to subdue various social equality groups as well as stifle people belonging to the Communist group.

On March 23, 1933 Hitler made use of the Enabling Act which allowed him to pass laws with the approval of Germany's Parliament or the President. Since Hitler wanted to get this law passed without delay He was able to stop Communist lawmakers from casting their votes. After it was passed, Hitler was allowed to govern as he wished and established his autocracy without any balance government.

The blame game for Germany's troubles is Jews and backstabbers, socialists and the ill-fated policies that came with the Weimar majority rule regime, Hitler and Hindenburg stood against each other during the 1932 presidential election. Hindenburg triumphed, however Hitler was able to win 37 per cent of the votes.

In July 14 million Germans were in favor of the Nazis in the new parliamentary elections which made Hitler's rally the largest in the Reichstag with 37 percent of seats.

The political turmoil that was brewing came through in a Reichstag political decision just four months after. The Nazis lost some members of the Reichstag however, it was the Communist Party picked up seats and drove a wide variety of crowds to support Hitler.

On January 30, 1933 President Hindenburg was reluctantly acquiesced to the selection of Hitler as the next Chancellor. Hitler pledged to observe closely the Weimar Constitution and structure a broad alliance government in order to solve the financial crisis.

The officials of the government exhorting Hindenburg to take over the country told him that they could manage the agitators from Bavaria. One of the political leaders said, "In two months we will have pushed

Hitler to the edge, so fast he'll be screaming."

Hitler however quickly outwitted other legislators. He persuaded Hindenburg to hold a second election, while governing through the decree. One of the orders restricted meetings between groups of the ideological variety and press access.

During the presidential race during the political race, a portion of the Reichstag was smashed to pieces. Hitler was accused of a conspiracy against the socialists. He also issued a "brief" order that suspended sacred rights to stifle the socialists.

In the month of March 1933, with nearly 6 million Germans unemployed In March 1933, the Nazi Party won 44 percent of Reichstag seats. With the assistance of traditional parties that were smaller, Hitler directed the majority of Germans to create a new parliament.

Hitler delivered an "Empowering Act" that required the Reichstag to transfer its lawmaking power to his office.

The law also permitted Hitler to ignore any agreement that was made by the previous government.

On the 23rd March 1933, the National Assembly was held in the Berlin drama theater to decide about the Enabling Act. With the streets lined with Nazi troops The Reichstag decided to abolish popular rule in Germany and to make Hitler the tyrant of"the "Third Reich."

It's hard to imagine a more unattainable figure who could take over Bismarck's throne and his fellow Hohenzollern sovereigns as well as the President Hindenburg than this single Austrian worker.

The birthplace in the Austro-German frontiers was intended to show a unique in that, even being a child, Hitler got fixated on the possibility that there would be no distinction between the two German-speaking communities and that both would have an important place in the same Reich. Such were the dependable and enduring nature of his beliefs that, at the age of 35, while in the confines of a German prison and was directing the writing which would later become the blueprint for The Third Reich, his first sentences were focused on the significance of his birthplace.

The night of November. 9-10th, 1938also popularly known as Kristallnacht the night of broken glass temples were set ablaze and stores were completely destroyed and Jewish homes were transformed into towns and urban areas across in the Third Reich. Police and firefighters held their ground with the intention of mediating in the event that neighboring "Aryan" properties resisted. In the following days, a lot of Jews were detained and rounded up within nearby facilities for corrections made-up penitentiaries, and a staggering 3000 people were deported for execution. Many families were evicted and lives ruined and livestock killed, just a handful of people of people killed, and a few hundred died. Germans as well as

Austrians of Jewish origin had no chance of survival in their home country. Some of them figured out ways to move abroad, leaving behind their homes and family members and those who were abandoned were later taken to death camps in the East.

The way we describe it in it's passive tone, illustrates the brutality committed against Jews. In addition, at this time of commemoration for tragic events it is logical to recall the individuals who were at fault. But, who was trustworthy? What kinds of exercises are we in a position to use today after the deadly attack on Jews at Pittsburgh's Pittsburgh Tree of Life place of worship?

The fear was inflicted upon those mentioned above, and was which was endorsed by Hitler and declassified by Goebbels. The most significant perpetrators were the undisputed Nazis - the dark booted SS and the earthy-colored shirted SA The optimistic Hitler Youth, the individuals of the affiliated associations who were showing insignias and collecting IDs.

But, the larger population's reaction led to the possibility -- and that's the factor that should be a cause for reflection in the present.

A vast number of common people such as ladies were involved in plundering and ravaging, picking up items thrown out onto the streets and making money from Jewish property confiscation. Young and old alike were able to humiliate Jews and whole classes of children being taken by their teachers to go to the sites of a raged worship place and to join the steering committees. Although some were encouraged through peer pressure, many students were able to accept the Nazi belief that "Jews are part of our history" and they saw it as "an perfect opportunity to care for the Jews."

In all likelihood there were those who said they felt "embarrassed by being German," and were in disapproval of the violence committed against people and the destruction of property. These remarks are documented in a variety of sources from the past and reports from onlookers across the Reich.

But, why did so many people not speak out in disapproval? Why did the those who were watching remain, in large part, silent, and not active?

To begin, there is the obvious issue with the state-mandated terror. The brutality began earlier in a state the political restrictions that were dynamic had been lifted, and in a state in a state where it's incredibly difficult to be a part of massive obstruction. Many political activists had recently left, often following early times of death camp, with some seeking to fight overseas. In the midst of a period of repression and repression, many residents were forced to remain silent. In the month of November 1938 some people worked out ways to provide aid in secret. Many who were afraid of harsh punishments, were left unaffected, no matter their feelings for the victims.

Given the circumstances that surround it and the underlying circumstances, there is an additional aspect that's more confusing about the long-term synchronicity with an overwhelmingly hostile atmosphere towards those who are deemed to be"the "other."

In 1938, after Hitler having been in his position for more than five years, the majority of non-Jewish Germans were forced to endure the Nazi system. Many were enthusiastic supporters to Hitler and his announced return to the public realm Many more were a part of to the Nazi political party (NSDAP) or affiliated associations due to entrepreneurial motives. Some bargained more cautiously and took on new roles in the open and muttering about differences in secret even though they were afraid of being judged for stepping beyond the line.

In the past, whether through long-standing or recently acquired conviction, or constrained congruity, people were able to exclude Jews from their activities in public as well as their social circles and even their recreational affiliations, and also lost contacts with Jews who were thrown off their job, and then forced to move out of their homes. Due to the growing physical and social divisions between networks "Aryans" (or people who were part of Hitler's flims "ace race" have were unable to communicate with "non-Aryans." In addition, with the growing apathy of their degrading situation was a lack of scholarly interest in their future.

This unintentional pattern of behavior, in reality, contributed to complicity.

The statement is clear it is clear that"The Nazi administration had posed the threat of a situation and began feasible measures, regardless whether they were enacted or savagery, in order to create an ethnically-defined "individuals in a particular area."

In general to whatever reason the people who were not banned contributed to creating a more colder condition that allowed it to be dreadful to all without any major distress or even any kind of intervention for the abusers.

The idea of "Third Reich" was first introduced at the time of 1922 by romantic moderate scholar and volkisch-patriot scholarly essayist Moeller van Cave Bruck. In his work, Das Dritte Reich (The Third Reich), Moeller imagined the rise of an opponent to liberalism, who was hostile to those who favored a Marxist Germanic Empire in which all social classes were to be considered as a result of the public's unity under the powerful magnetic "Fuhrer" (pioneer). The Moeller's "Third Reich" referenced two previous Germanic Empires including Charlemagne's middle age Frankish Empire in the middle age Frankish Empire and also The German Empire that was under Hohenzollern.

Prussian Hohenzollern regime (1871-1918).

Chapter 2: What Was The Motivation Behind Adolf Hitler?

His birthplace was an Austrian town that was close to the border between Germany and Austria. Alois the father of Adolf Hitler was an official of the state customs service throughout his life. His son spent the bulk of his teenage years in Linz which was the capital in Upper Austria.

In a bid to not follow in the footsteps of his father's career as a federal employee and he began fighting in a school that was optional and, at the end, he dropped out. Alois passed away in 1903 and Adolf was determined to fulfill his dream of becoming an artist. However the next day, he was removed out of Vienna's Academy of Fine Arts.

When the death of his mom, Klara who died 1908 Hitler was forced to move to Vienna and began to make the money by painting scenic landscapes and landmarks as well as selling his work. Insular and lonely, Hitler got inspired by legislation during his time in Vienna and formulated a lot of the concepts that would later form the Nazi beliefs.

The year 1913 was the time that Hitler relocated in 1913 to Munich within the German area of Bavaria. As World War I broke out in the following summer In 1913, he asked the Bavarian Lord to be allowed to join a rescue infantry regiment.

The convoy was transported in October 1914 and transferred to Belgium, Hitler served all through the Great War and won two medals of valor, including the rare Iron Cross First Class, that he wore until the very end of his life.

Hitler was twice wounded during the conflict. He was wounded in the leg during Somme in 1916, and was also blinded during the British gas attack close to Ypres during 1918. After about a month of recovery, he was in a medical facility located in Pasewalk near the northwestern part of Berlin and the news broke of the peace treaty and the destruction of Germany during World War I.

Similar to many other Germans, Hitler came to accept that the country's destruction, which could not be attributed to the Allies as much as to insufficiently dedicated "deceivers" at home--a myth that was to undermine the post-war Weimar Republic and set up Hitler's rise.

When Hitler returned to Munich in the latter part of 1918 He joined the small German Workers' Party that aimed to unite the interests of common working class with a firm German patriotic spirit.

In one of Hitler's masterful strokes, the newly named National Socialist German Workers Party (also known as the Nazi Party, embraced a version of the Hakenkreuz's outdated image, which featured a cross to represent its emblem. Its white hover, Hitler's symbol could become a frightening image of a representative in the years ahead.

In the years before 1921's end, Hitler led the developing Nazi Party, profiting by inevitable disputes between government officials from the Weimar Government and by constantly refusing to abide by the conditions that were part of the Versailles Treaty. Many former military officials who were unhappy in Munich joined the Nazis including Ernst Rohm, who selected the "solid arm" squads, also known informally as Sturmabteilung (SA)the Sturmabteilung (SA),that Hitler employed to protect groups and slay rivals.

Brew Hall Putsch

On the evening on November 8 on 1923, a group of people from the SA and other groups pushed through a massive beer hall, where another conservative leader was manning the crowd. With a gun, Hitler declared the beginning of unrest in the streets and then drove protesters into the heart of Munich and were involved in a dispute with police. Hitler fled, but was later captured as were his fellow rebellious pioneers. Although it was a disaster but The Beer Hall Putsch built up Hitler as a figure in the public eye.

The author of his autobiography

In 1924, when he was charged with the treason of his country the sentence imposed by Hitler was five years of prison. But he was released within nine months of the comforts at Landsberg Castle. In that time the writer began writing the novel which would eventually be called "Mein Kampf" ("My Struggle").

In this, Hitler developed the nationalistic anti-Semitic and nationalist views he begun to develop in Vienna in his late twenties and began to spread designs for Germany and the world he attempted to develop when he gained the reins.

Hitler was to finish his second book of "Mein Kampf" following his release, after he was freed from Berchtesgaden's mountain air. The book was a success at first, but it would become Germany's most sought-after publication following the Bible after Hitler's rise to power. In 1940, the book had sold about 6 million copies.

Hitler's next book, "The Zweites Buch," was published in 1928 and included his plans for a global strategy. But, due to the pathetic beginning deals in "Mein Kampf," the book was published following the death of Hitler. The original English version from "The Zweites Book" didn't appear until 1962, and it was published under the name "Hitler's The Secret Book."

Aryan Race:

Obsessed with race and the potential for the possibility of ethnic "virtue," Hitler saw an eminent plan to put the supposed "Aryan race" in the forefront.

According to him his Volk (the German public) would find its truest manifesto not in a fair or parliamentary Government, but rather in an unrivalled pioneer known as a Fuhrer.

"Mein Kampf" also emphasized the need of Lebensraum (or the living area) to satisfy the predetermination of the film, Germany should assume control over areas to the east that were previously inhabited by "substandard" Slavic groups--including Austria as well as in particular the Sudetenland (Czechoslovakia), Poland and Russia.

It is the Schutzstaffel (SS)

When Hitler quit prison the financial aid program had been reestablished an aid well-known to those in the Weimar Republic, and backing for causes that were traditionally supported like Nazism seemed to have all the hallmarks of disappearing.

Through the next few years, Hitler disappeared and tried to restructure and redesign in the Nazi Party. He established his Hitler Youth Hitler Youth to sort out teenagers and created the Schutzstaffel (SS) an easier alternative to the SA.

The members of the SS were dressed in dark clothing and made a vow of non-stop loyalty to Hitler. (After 1929 under the direction under the leadership of Heinrich Himmler, the SS would form from a group of a minimum of 200 people a force that would engulf Germany as well as threaten the rest of the involved Europe in World War II.)

The SS was established in 1925 "Schutzstaffel," German for "Defensive Echelon,"" was initially constituted to act as Nazi Party pioneer Adolf Hitler's (1889-1945) personal protectors and then became among the most formidable and hated associations of Nazi Germany. Heinrich Himmler (1900-45), a fierce adversary of Semites as was Hitler was the top leader of the Schutzstaffel or SS in 1929. He also expanded its mission and size. At the time of World War II (1939-45) The SS included nearly 250,000 members, and diverse developments, engaged in activities that ranged from knowledge-based tasks to the running of Nazi concentration camps. In the post-war Nuremberg trials and trials, the SS was considered to be an organization that committed crimes due to the immediate role it played in atrocities.

The sources of SS

It was in 1921 that Adolf Hitler became the first leader of a new political organization known as"the National Socialist German Workers' (Nazi) Party. The group promoted a slew of German patriotic sentiment and a hostility towards Semitism and was disappointed by the Treaty of Versailles, the 1919 peace settlement that ended World War I (1914-18) and demanded a variety of concessions from Germany. Hitler claimed that Jews as well as Marxists of causing Germany's problems. He promoted the idea of the existence of an Aryan "ace race."

Prior to the end of 1921, Hitler had his private military force, called the "Sturmabteilung" ("Assault Division") (also known as SA who were called tempest troopers or earthy-colored shirt (for the color of their attire). The SA was together with Hitler in public appearances and was present in his fiery speeches in which he urged his allies to carry out brutality against Jews as well as his political adversaries.

It was in 1925 that Hitler asked for the creation of the Schutzstaffel. It was a unit which was separate from, yet closely linked to, the SA. The SS was initially composed of eight members, each of them was dependent on keeping an eye on Hitler as well as other important Nazis. Julius Schreck (1898-1936), an unwavering Hitler adherent, was transformed into the SS's top leader. In the following time, Schreck frequently was possible had a fake mustache that resembled Hitler's was replaced by Joseph Berchtold (1897-1962). Erhard Heiden (1901-33) was appointed the head of The SS from 1927. In the was the same year that SS personnel were warned not to take part in political discussions and required to declare their unwavering loyalty towards Hitler and confidently acknowledge Heiden as their prophet unrivaled.

Heinrich Himmler, Architect of the SS

On the 6th January 1929 Hitler announced that he would make Heinrich Himmler an officer of the SS that had more than 300 people. Himmler as a fellow Nazi, and like Hitler was a fierce antagonist of Semites and Semites, was the host of in 1923 the Nazi Gathering in 1923. He also, at the end of the day, was tapped to fill the role of Hitler's opportunistic publicity boss. Himmler decided to segregate from the SS away from SA and transform the SS into an elite power that was larger and more powerful than the SA and finally alter the role of the SS within that of the Nazi Party.

Under the guidance of Himmler under his direction, under Himmler's direction, the SS evolved over the next four years into an elite paramilitary organization. In order to be SS-like future members needed to show that they were not Jewish and also agree to marry clearly with their official bosses in their consent. The military's training sessions were intense, as if they were the highest level for the Nazi Party. In all other respects they were expected to show dedication and devotion toward their belief in the Nazi ideal, set specific concerns aside, and carry out their obligations with determination and as a unit that was durable. These ideals were evident in the SS statement: "Unwaveringness is my honor."

Eva Braun

Hitler was a major part of his life in Berchtesgaden during this time as did his step-sister, Angela Raubal, and her two young daughters often traveled with Hitler. After Hitler became enthralled by his gorgeous blonde niece Geli Raubal insatiable attraction drove her to take her own life in 1931.

Infuriated by his misfortunes, Hitler would consider Geli as the main romantic endeavor in his entire life. In the end, he began an intimate relationship of Eva Braun, a right shop worker from Munich however, he would not get married to her.

The Great Depression that started in 1929 weakened the strength of Weimar

Republic. In his determination to use political power to control his rebellion, Hitler developed Nazi help in the ranks of German preservationists, which included businesses, armed forces and even modern pioneers.

Hitler was not the first to initiate the disdain for Jews. Jews throughout Europe have been victims of mistreatment and separation from during the Middle Ages, regularly for very specific motives. Christians believed that being confident was being a deviant. Jews however, were required to convert in order to be allowed to be employed in certain occupations. In the 19th century, religion took on a less important part. It was evident from the debates on the differences between different races and groups of people. It was possible that Jews were unusual people, compared to Germans For instance, they was accepted. In fact there was a possibility that even Jews who converted to Christianity were still unique because of their bloodline.

The reason Hitler was so smug for Jews isn't exactly clear. When he wrote Mein Kampf, he portrayed his rise to hatred of Jews as a result of a lengthy individual struggle. In the sense that anyone can tell his hatred of everything Jewish was as normal in his time of living and painting at the age of Vienna (1908-1913). Many antiquarians believe that Hitler was thinking of this explanation in the past. He could have used it to safeguard those who were not in line with his mentality in the end. Somehow or other, Hitler came into contact with a smattering of bigoted ideas in his early years. The extent to which he shared these views at the time, isn't certain. If he was averse to Jews when he lived in Vienna the city, his views was not yet firmly established into an unmistakable view. The most loyal buyers of his art in Vienna was one who was a Jew, Samuel Morgenstern.

The evidence is clear that two Austrian government officials had a profound impact on Hitler's thinking. One of them,

Georg Ritter von Schonerer (1842-1921) was an ardent German patriotic citizen. He was adamant that the German-speaking districts of Austria-Hungary must fall within the German domain. He also believed that Jews were never completely German citizens. In the second instance, the Viennese municipal chairman Karl Lueger (1844-1910), Hitler realized the ways in which discrimination against Jews as well as social changes could prove fruitful. Through Mein Kampf, Hitler adulated Lueger as the 'best German civic chairperson ever.' After Hitler was elected at the beginning of 1933, he enacted similar ideas as a routine event.

The First World War assumed a crucial role in Hitler's life. It provided the life of Hitler, that was mostly unproductive up to this moment, a cause. He was enlisted in the German military that were fighting France, England, and Russia together with The Austro-Hungarian Empire. While he did not see much activities, he received an award for bravery displayed. When

Germany was defeated on November 11, 1918 Hitler had been in the medical emergency clinic for the military. He suffered eye injuries from the toxin gas attack in Belgium. He was confined to his bed and listened to the German updates on acquiescence and was pushed into an acute emergency. He wrote that "all was dark as I looked up.' After a stumble, he made his way back to his quarters and buried his head with a pillow and cover.

The German beating was difficult to be accepted by certain Germans The German thrashing was a challenge for some Germans, and Hitler also. In traditional moderate and patriot circles, the "betray myth was accepted as a common belief. Based on this fantasy, Germany did not lose the war in the battlefield however, it was through treachery on the front at home. In the home front, Jews, Social Democrats, and Communists were blamed. The notions of partiality regarding the role of the Jews during the war were untrue. A review conducted by the

German Government revealed quite a bit. There were more than 100,000 German and Austrian Jews had battled for their country. Otto Frank, who had participated in the Somme's Conflict in 1916, was just one.

With the backdrop of transformation and brutality Hitler's discrimination against Jews became increasingly extremist. He was not often explicit that he didn't support violent and uncontrolled massacres (upheavals of protest against Jewish violence). He instead advocated for discrimination towards Jews by their mind.' It had to be legal and could eventually result in the 'expulsion' of Jews. At the time in August of 1920 Hitler declared that the Jews against germs. He said that the spread of infections was not manageable, except by eliminating their root causes. The Jews' influence will never be eradicated without removing the source of its influence and its source, the Jew in our middle, he stated. These thoughts of extremes were to be the basis for the mass murder of Jews in the 1940s.

Hitler was adamant about the Jews for everything that was wrong with the world. Germany was weak and deteriorating due to the 'Jewish effect.' According to Hitler in his speech, the Jews wanted to dominate the world. In addition they were not able to spare any moment to employ every possible means that included free enterprise. This is why Hitler made use of the present bias which linked the Jews with influence based on money and financial profit. Hitler was not affrighted with the apparent inconsistencies within his argument. He believed the view that socialists were Jewish co-operation, since the most prominent element of the chiefs of socialists was Jewish in that, to an extent, Jews were social democrats. The notion of 'Jewish socialism had a dreadful effects in the war with and the Soviet Union that began in 1941. The detainees and the populace of war were treated brutally with the Germans.

Hitler considered the entire world an endless struggle between different groups of people. He separated the whole population into low and high races. The Germans were part of the higher population groups, and the Jews were among the lowest. The author also had in-depth thoughts on various categories. He also had detailed thoughts about different groups. Slavic populace, for instance was seen as substandard, and was destined to be controlled. Hitler believed his German public was required to be stable, if they were "unadulterated.' In the end, people who had genetic diseases were considered to be dangerous.

They included those who were mentally or physically disabled as well as drunkards and hopeless criminals. After the Nazis were in control their thoughts, they prompted strict disinfection and murder of individuals.

Chapter 3: The Early Stages Of Being

The theory that Hitler was able to formulate during his time in Vienna and had never forgotten that the best way to control a progressive growth was to align it with a section of the amazing organizations within the State - has been put into execution exactly as he believed. The President, with the support of the Army and traditionalists, elected the position of Chancellor. His political power, though amazing it was, as a matter of fact not completely. It gave these three power sources that put him in the outside world and in at times and awed by what was happening in the National Socialist development.

So, Hitler's first task was to remove their control quickly, making his own group the "selective ace" for the state, and then in the presence of a brutal state and its police force and its police, end the Nazi tensions. He was in his office for only a short time before making his first unambiguous move, revealing a trap to his inscrutable mild "captors" and putting in motion a series of events that he initiated or controlled, and that towards the end of a half-year would result in the complete Nazification of Germany. Additionally, his rise as the status of the Reich's despot was a bind and made Germany defederalized to the extent that it was never before in German history.

Five hours after his confirmation, on the night of 1933 Hitler had his very first meeting with the bureau. These minutes that turned up in Nuremberg amid the vast amount of uncovered mystery records reveal how quickly and effectively Hitler with the help of the clever Goering began to take his moderates to the races. Hindenburg was the one who had appointed Hitler to be the president, not a president-appointed bureau, however, he was dependent on the majority of the Reichstag. But those who were the Nazis along with the Nationalists who were the two main parties that met in the legislative chamber, held only 247 seats of 583 seats in the parliament and, as a result they didn't possess the majority. In order to achieve this they needed the backing by the Center Party with its 70 seats. In the early days of the new administration, Hitler had dispatched Goering to meet with Centrist head of the party, but now he informed his bureau that Center wanted "certain compromises."

Hugenberg, a sluggish brain man with a lot of accomplishments protested, shifting his frustration to the legislative. But, the new rules regarding Nazis that have the State's assets to back them could earn an overwhelming majority in surveys. They could also be in a position to manage his administration and his moderate comrades. Hitler proposed essentially smothering all of the Communist Party; with its 100 seats eliminated and it would be the Nazis as well as the Nationalists will have a bigger percentage. Hitler was not going to go that far in that time and finally agreed to meet together with Center Party pioneers the next morning. If the talks were in vain the bureau would ask for new races.

Hitler quickly made them unprofitable. In response to his request the Center head Monsignor Kaas offered as the basis for discussion an exhaustive list of questions which included an interest Hitler will guarantee to manage in the best way possible. But, Hitler, deceiving both Kaas and his bureau personnel responded to the question claim that it was the Center had set unrealistic expectations and there was no chance of a consensus. He therefore suggested that the president disband the Reichstag and call for new elections. The two of them Hugenberg and Papen had been in the crossfire, however, after a clear affirmation by the Nazi chief, that the bureau would remain unaltered regardless of how the race were conducted, they agreed to comply with him. The date of the next race was set for March 5.

In the most recent, free political contest, Germany was to have the Nazi Party utilize all the administration's vast assets to gain votes. Goebbels was delighted. "Presently it is easy," he wrote in his diary on February 3 "to keep fighting as we have access to all the resources from the government. Press and radio are both at our disposal. We can arrange a grand opus of targeted public relations. In addition This time around, typically there's no shortage of cash."

The massive managers of money happy with the new administration that was planning to put the laborers that had been cleared out into their proper place and leave the board to manage its own organizations however it wanted and wanted to settle. They agreed in a conference on the 20th of February at the Goering's Reichstag Presidential Palace. In the palace the Dr. Schacht went about as host and Goering and Hitler laid out the plan to a small number of Germany's most powerful magnates including Krupp of Bohlen who was enthusiastic Nazi in the short-term, Bosch as well as Schnitzler who were from I. G. Farben as well as Voegler at the top from the United Steel Works.

Hitler began a long debate by offering a slap to the industrialists. "Private enterprise," he stated, "cannot be maintained during the times of popular government. It is feasible only if the people have a solid idea of the power and moral character . . . The majority of the items we use today are a result of the war of the pick . . . It is important to remember that all benefits of culture should be presented in a manner that is characterized by a grip."

He promised the money-managers that they was going to "dispense from" the Marxists as well would he reestablish his Wehrmacht (the latter was of unusual enthusiasm for such organizations).

In The Great Depression, paper inclusion was the primary source of information about world political events and the need for papers to gather informing, communicating, and presenting information to the general public. Papers did not only transmit information, but it also affected the general public's mind and examined the information it published, depending on the style, language choice, and presentation as well as shedding an understanding of the way that global news brought about change for those in American public. The announcement of Hitler's ascent to power within Germany and the extremely reshaping strategies of the initial Nazi system provide a unique method of assessing the continuous improvement would be seen as unlucky today, with careless endorsements, or even sporadic worries from the paper distributors at the time. This article will examine Adolf Hitler and the Nazi Party in Germany in the pages that appeared in The Seattle Times, one of the city's most important newspapers in 1933. When Hitler gained control, The Seattle Times was initially reluctant to study his Nazi Party, and printed many articles that reassured readers with his calming issues, while writing about the enemies of Jewish oppression. At the end of the year it was likely that The Times become worried about the growing power of Hitler and reveal some insight into the apparent lack of concern about Nazi suppression during the initial lengthy periods of Hitler's regime?

In the month of January, 1933 Adolf Hitler turned into an international celebrity as the spokesman in Germany in of the Nazi party. The Seattle Times ran numerous stories about Germany. It gathered reactions to the events that took place there. A section of the news conveys a passion while others convey the information with a less subtle and sloppy manner.

According to The Times' article on March 23 titled "Hitler granted 4-year term as Supreme Ruler" Hitler was quoted as saying "No massive change in comparative measurements has been achieved with such a consistent control, resulting in very little destruction like the revolution we are experiencing." The motivation behind Hitler's declaration is obvious: to assure to the world that he was managing for the people and that there was no necessity for violence. But, The Times' inclusion began to examine Hitler's statement. Nearly to the limit of March's most extreme There was a plethora of news articles that discussed what was happening to Jews throughout Germany. On the 24thof March, two the articles were titled "England is enraged by reports about Nazi violence" as well as "Eastern Jews are Exiled of Germany."

Two days later on the 26th of July The articles were handed out with the names "[BritishBritish Jews boycott German Goods," and "Abuse of Jews is not permitted." The titles were enough to cause a stir and shook doubt about Hitler's previous declarations of peace. In addition, the titles of these articles convey some specific message. But, the manner in which they were put together in the same location (inside the specific issue) also demonstrated The Times' acknowledgment of the significance of certain events.

Similar to the way that the news coverage began to turn towards concerns about Hitler and his regime, viewers of The Seattle Times were, at times, comforted The same time that stories about Jewish oppression were published through the press. On the 26th of March the newspaper published another article, that was titled "Hitler was praised." The article explained "Washington copyist's interruption in order to give acknowledgement of the remark made at Herr Hitler, Germany's bubbly Chancellor." It dispelled any fear which could have resulted from news reports concerning Jewish discrimination and secluded Hitler's power from the German's infringing upon its Jewish and dissenting residents' rights. With the use of words like bubbly, with an extremely certain meaning the writer of this article compelled the reader to look in favor of Adolf Hitler. The Seattle Times likewise distributed pieces that seemed to comfort readers over the previous day's report: "Germany Tells US Catholics that Jews are Safe." The report stated the fact that Germany's German Foreign Minister informed Cardinal Boston that, in light of the extent of the alleged discrimination against German Jews, "I ask to ensure that the allegations have any basis." In the next day's edition, The Seattle Times ventured into the extreme of to claim that "there is no way to end the abusing of Jews throughout Germany" in addition to "In our country in any case the official positions of government are dependable and fair. Their affirmation that there is any racial discrimination in Germany and that there will never be could be based on." Again, The Seattle Times was encouraging its readers following the publication of stories about barbarities, that all was fine in Germany and that there was no reason to emphasize.

The practice of announcing restriction of the Nazis on Jews and then announcing consoling articles continued throughout the spring. Just a few days after the publication that stated it was "no discrimination based on race," The Times' March 31st issue stated: "Nazis Expel Jewish Judges." The article's first page was entitled "Hitler The War on Judah to be Extreme and Universal: Virtual Elimination of Race from the Economic Life of Reich Starts in Earnest Tomorrow morning." The article clarified that Nazis had barred the demonstrators (Jews, Communists, and Marxists) from a specialized criminal courts. The suppression of nonconformists was a move towards complete control. This should be extremely troubling for the citizens of Seattle when they watched these developments unfold, particularly when they read the following line: "new government announcement... described the actions towards Jews as the beginning of a battle against all of the Jewish race in the world."

Some issues of April contained news that addressed these concerns of a lack of freedom, while various articles argued the opposite. A news article from April 1 described the beginning of the Jewish boycott that began in Germany and lasted for a period of time during which Germans were able to boycott Jewish work spaces in a statement that read, "There were such numerous horrifying perspectives to the event." The word"shocking" has a particular negative meaning, and it was certainly shocking for the reader. The April 3 issue substantiated the unfitting impact, saying that "starting 12 noon, nobody will be allowed to leave German territory without permission from the government." The event prompted protesters, like Jews and detainees of their legislative bodies. But, in spite of the bleak style, this piece was not astonished by the emphasis. It was almost as if The Seattle Times did not even have a clue what to make of the news and, consequently readers could have been in the same situation.

A powerful piece that appeared in The Seattle Times on April 7, of the magazine highlighted the disparities in information The Seattle Times revealed and its general faith on Hitler's system. The article contained an email from an anonymous reader entitled "Our Weakness and ignorance."

The writer argued that "In the current publication that appeared in The Times, there seemed an article titled "No Persecution The essayist of which showed a level of confidence with Adolf Hitler." The article then asked "Does the Times even think for the German government will concede that there was some sort of violations or that our discretionary representatives to Berlin will be informed about the events that take place in the background?" Furthermore, the article the article was closed "To say that Hitler will not tolerate any form of oppression consciously committed to the Jews indicates that the author of the piece is utterly ignorant of the historical background of German political system." This was an important article that appeared in The Times since it was written by a person who was able to clearly draw attention to the contradictory inclusion in The Seattle Times. The writer tried to expose readers of the Seattle Times, to what was really going on, and possibly increase the sense of dread towards the Nazis.

In spite of the current reader's letter of dissent, The Seattle Times distributed articles with a contrasting tone. For instance, a piece that appeared on April 23 described fascism as "Simple Interludes" or "compromise[sbetween a flurry of frequently wasteful, but consistently praised traditional rule and the institution by monarchy." The 23rd of April the entire page contained an interview together with Emil Lengyel, the writer of the book titled Hitler. In the discussion, "Mr. Lengyel... doesn't believe his belief that Hitler... is going to begin as rough a course as many people fear. He is aware that Hitler will provide Germany an administrative system that is not far off the course of action." Both articles had the impression of comfort. It seemed like The Times was endeavoring to stop the rumblings in Seattle through the distribution of consoling news and trying to reduce the scope of restrictions of the Nazis, perhaps because of a lack of anxiety for Jewish people.

In May 16 the article included the words "Incapacitate, Roosevelt Pleads!" While the article stated the fact that Roosevelt did not mention an individual country, the fact is that he was in fact in charge of this appeal to German militarism. Two days later, following their previous example, The Times printed an article that reiterated the faith in Nazi Germany's peaceful determination. The article was titled "All Germany to Support Hitler in a Peaceful Stand," expressed that "the whole German country is today energized by the legislature with seriousness in ensuring the world that her consecrated the goals of peace are not achievable." In a particular way, The Times' inclusion was a follow-up on the political development of Hitler and he didn't do anything to make a nation administrator nation administrators, nations violent and threatening actions with explanations of the peace and authenticity of his group's expectations. The story continued On May 30 an article entitled: "Germany Says 'Hands Off in Jewish Policy." Hitler asked to the League of Nations to "keep its fingers off the topic of Germany's treatment of Jews." Anyone who read this article would be extremely skeptical of this statement to convey an "do ask-don't say" manner of addressing Nazism. Nazi treatment of Jews. Other articles about the inexplicably limiting nature of Hitler's system were published over the next four months.

In the long stretch of June, July, August in September and June, Hitler began to use his extreme muscles fully. In June 19, an article that read "Nazi Government may reprimand children," there was a statement that read, "Hitler has harshly cautioned German guardians that their children will be removed and placed under the administration's control in the event that they do not grow up to be noted Nazis."

on the 14th of August, a man who was from America was arrested. United States was condemned to six months in prison because he was believed to be thinking of Hitler as an Czech Jew. In addition, on the 19th of August the newspaper published an article that was titled "When in Berlin do as the Nazis Do," recounting the account of another American man who was beaten by soldiers of Hitler's in Berlin for not saluting Nazi soldiers that were walking around the city. Finally, a piece was published on September 1st was entitled "Hitler was treated as King at the Nazi Congress." These articles informed those living in Seattle about the expectations Hitler had in Germany as well as around the world. If there were any doubts about the possibility that Hitler would rule with an "iron grasp," they would have been answered in the final spring's news articles. The most recent two long periods in 1933 show the same type of activity.

For a considerable period in the past, the USSR was engaged in discussions in talks with Britain and France and had pledged to defend Poland in the event that Germany struck, in order to create an alliance of three paths against Nazi hostility. Germany along with the USSR even though they had signed an agreement on financial matters on the day prior. At present, Hitler required a political solution and Molotov claimed he was "energetically was invited." The plans to fight for war were in limbo as European forces considered forming an alliance to fight Germany, Hitler could not conceal his desperation. "The tensions between Germany and Poland has become very severe," he cautioned Stalin. "An emergency may emerge quickly."

Then, Stalin's reaction came out 27 hours following the factthat he had sent Ribbentrop the way of Moscow.

On the 23rd of August 1939 Ribbentrop arrived with prepared requests to Hitler to organize. A purely discretionary invasion like this could have been astonished only a few days earlier. In the past, Nazis and Soviets were mortal enemies on opposing sides of the philosophical spectrum, who used the other's hatred to fuel their nefarious systems. Today, Realpolitik bested philosophy. Following the Germans accuse Czechoslovakia earlier in the year of that it was infringing on the Munich Agreement, Stalin scrutinized the motivations for both the British as well as the French to defeat the Nazis. The Soviets found an agreement with the Germans attractive considering the fact that they were at that moment engaged in a fierce fighting on their east front against the Japanese while they were also aware that the Red Army was as yet weak from

Stalin's purge of its highest officials in 1937 and 1938.

It was so sudden that the defrost among them, that all five banners with insignia were hurriedly taken to the air terminal to greet Ribbentrop at his appearance to be removed away from Soviet film studios making anti-Nazi films. While seated on the arranging table in the Kremlin the unpretentious German priest offered an elaborate introduction of friendship between the two countries. Even a tyrant who was a rogue realized that reality has to be twisted in a certain way before it snaps. "The Soviet government could not suddenly give the public the affirmations of friendship after having been encased with compost buckets from The Nazi government for quite a while," Stalin stated, according to the book by William Shirer The Rise and Fall of the Third Reich.

Although Soviet negotiations between those of the British and French were delayed for a considerable duration, it took just hours to negotiate an agreement that was negotiated with Germans. The conference "started and concluded with enthusiasm and to show how skilled these dictators were," the New York Times editorialized. The Molotov-Ribbentrop Pact was officially dubbed which is also often referred to in the Hitler-Stalin Pact, the peace agreement was clear and unambiguous. Both nations pledged for a lengthy period "to refrain from any act of aggression, any forceful action, and any attack on each other, whether in isolation or in conjunction with other forces."

While a huge, surrounded image taken of Vladimir Lenin looked down harshly at the smoke-filled room, Ribbentrop and Molotov joined their signatures on the agreement. A smiling Stalin was as radiant as the Crimean sparkling wine that the Russian leader offered in a frank salute to Hitler. "I am aware of that the German nation loves it's Fuhrer," he said. "I would therefore prefer to celebrate the health of his father."

The understanding resulted in that the pen's second stroke brushed against the paper and a rare conciliatory state that was a reflection of how overwhelmed Hitler felt. Ribbentrop described a frightened Hitler in his retreat on the mountains at Bavaria with the announcement. "That is an asterisk," said a delighted Hitler who could then begin to strike Poland not frightened of a Soviet intercession or an armed conflict that had devastated Germany during World War I

"The terrible news swept across all of humanity like blast" Winston Churchill later composed. It was also the news people were thinking about, as despite the peace treaty that was signed, it was reported that the Nazis and Soviets were locked in a secret agreement that was just coming to an end after World War II. Both nations used a cutting knife to Poland in the direction of Poland, with the Germans choosing the more important cutting edge to the west.

Prior to when Ribbentrop quit Ribbentrop's Kremlin, Stalin pulled him away. "The Soviet Government pays attention to the new agreement in a very special way," the despot stated and could rely that he kept his "promise of respect of honor" that Soviet Union would not deceive its accomplices." Stalin probably thought about whether Hitler believed the same due to the Chancellor's willingness to accept any Soviet demands, as well as his inclination to repeatedly breaking agreements.

"Our settlement means that the top European forces have agreed to avert the risk of war and live in peace," Molotov told the Supreme Soviet prior to it approving the agreement in the evening on August 31. After a few hours more than one million German soldiers crossed the border of Poland. World War II had started. Within a few months after the war, the Soviets attacked the eastern region of Poland with the intention of protecting its inhabitants from Germans. After a few months Stalin's soldiers entered Poland's Baltics along with Bessarabia.

Prior to when the Peace deal before the signing of the peace agreement, President Franklin D. Roosevelt cautioned Stalin that "it was certain that night followed day that once Hitler defeated France the Germans would turn their attention to Russia and that it was the Soviets having a chance right away." These words were shrewd in the event that in June of 1941 Hitler in a singular manner broke off his contract with Stalin and launched the most devastating ever attack in the history of the war.

The Legion Freies Indien, alluded to in casual terms as"the Indische Legion ("Indian Legion") or, alternatively, similarly by"the Tiger Legion and the Azad Hind Fauj (Hindi: "Free India Army") is an Indian military unit formed in World War II in Germany. It was initially established in 1941, and then was a part of with the

German Army (Wehrmacht Heer) and , later, in August 1944, was added to the Waffen-SS. The Army was designed to act with the Indian Freedom Force. It was conceived via Subhas Chandra Bose, director of the Indian National Congress and an important pioneer in the process of Indian autonomy movement and helped establish the Army upon his arrival in Berlin in 1941 after having escaped British House arrest in India. The soldiers who enlisted were Indian understudy volunteers who were living in Germany in the early days as well as a few were Indian prisoner of war (POWs) were captured from Erwin Rommel during his North Africa Campaign. Later, it would draw more of Indian POWs who were enlisted as volunteers.

While it was an armed group which would serve as the way for a German-Indian joint invasion of British India's western boondocks thousands of legionnaires were sent to the eastern part of Iran as part of 'Activity Bajadere in order to conquer India by way of Baluchistan and inflict harm on the British in the hope of a feared public revolt. The majority of Indian Legion soldiers were just never positioned in Europe mostly in non-battle obligation and starting from Netherlands until Atlantic Wall obligations in France until the French Allied invasion. A tiny amount of the uninvited, including the officers and the administration corps, was transferred into Azad Hind ("Free India") following its arrangement and witnessed activity during the Indian National Army's Burma Campaign. In Italy the unit experienced combat in the face of British as well as Polish soldiers, and was a fervent supporter of the enemies of sectarian duties in 1944.

When the time of the Third Reich surrender in 1945 In 1945, the remaining Indian Legion soldiers attempted to travel to an impartial Switzerland across the Alps. But, their efforts became futile since American or French soldiers intercepted them and eventually returned them to

India to be tried for indictments of treason.

Due to the chaos the preliminary proceedings were not completed. Due to the chaos that Indians who fought the Axis created among the regular population and the army in British India, the Indian Legion individual's preliminaries were not complete.

The Third Reich was a police state characterized by self-assertive arrest and detention of philosophers and political opponents in inhumane prisons.

After the revision of "defensive care" (Schutzhaft) in 1933, police power was without legal restrictions. In Nazi formulation, the term "defensive care" meant the capturing, without legal basis, of the system's real and expected opponents. "Defensive guardianship" detainees weren't restricted to the standard jail structure but were in death camps, under the SS's arbitrary authority (Schutzstaffel were the top watchmen for

Schutzstaffel, the first-class watchmen of Nazi State).

Jewish legal experts gathered to request consent to be present before the Berlin courts' watchful eyes. Jewish lawyers gathered to request permission to be present in front of the Berlin courts' watchful eyes.

New guidelines laid out within the Aryan Paragraph (a sequence of laws enacted in April 1933 to expel Jews from various sections of society and State) allowed only 35 Jews to be present under the supervision by the courts. Berlin, Germany, April 11 33.

The Third Reich has been known as a double-state since the normative legal framework was in sync to Hitler as well as the subjective police aggression. In reality, since most of the areas of public life after the Nazi rise to power in 1933 in 1933, there was a German system of equity worked via "coordination" (arrangement in accordance with Nazi goals). All affiliations with experts associated with the equity group merged to form one organization, the National Socialist League of German Jurists. Then, in April of 1933 Hitler introduced one of his most frequent anti-ethnic laws, which removed Jewish as well as Socialist appointed officials such as legal advisors, legal advisers, and Court officials out of their posts. Additionally The Academy of German Law and Nazi legitimate scholars, such as Carl Schmitt, upheld the Nazification of German law, removing it of "Jewish influence." Judges were instructed to allow "sound assumptions about society" (gesundes Volksempfinden) determine their decisions.

Hitler decided to extend the political credibility of the courts. In 1933, he established superior courts across Germany to decide politically sensitive cases. Unsatisfied with the "not faultworthy rulings of the Supreme Court (Reichsgericht) in the Reichstag Fire Trial, Hitler demanded the creation of the

People's Court (Volksgerichtshof) in Berlin in 1934 in order to try the conspiracy theory and other "political instances." In the era of Roland Freisler, the People's Court was deemed vital to the Nazi system of dread, condemning a multitude of people as "Volk vermin" and putting thousands of others to be executed in the case of "Volk Treason." The first and final condemnation of those accused of involvement with the July Plot as well as the plan for the execution of Hitler during July 1944, was totally absurd.

The evidence shows that a shrewd change to the constitution, based on the rule of revision alone could be legal without consolidating the entire time or re-instating later the adjustments that was expected by the resolution of the constitution's text. However the fact that this Enabling Act was not just an adjustment to some or a few of the provisions to the Constitution. It was an absolute reversal of the existing order in place at the time. The fundamental alteration of the entire sacred structure, the term "complete change" of"complete amendment" in French and Swiss law, goes beyond the normal altering organs' ward. It declared "first in the constitution's constituent intensity of the entire German nation." ."'" While the majority of the sacred legal advisers prior to 1933, who allowed this clause in connection with the customary and necessary changes to the constitution, continued to insist on the importance of Article 7620 in all amendments of any kind. It's easy to overlook however that this National Socialist faction spoke to just a tiny minority. In spite of including the votes of its ally that is that of the German National People's Party, it was largely below the generally accepted standard for a shifting majority.

Another test of the reliability in the Enabling Act is even more authentic. The Act was passed with 494 votes in the Reichstag and was later amended according to the Constitution's Article 76.

However, 81 members from the banned Communist section were not permitted to attend the event, nor were 120 members belonging to those who belong to the Social Democrats. Additionally, 92 people of members of the Catholic Center, the Social Democrats as well as small "splinter parties" voting to support the protest were prevented from casting the vote in a fair and free manner. The demonstrators that was released by the government entered the legislative chamber and the vote took place within an incredibly hostile atmosphere of intimidation and fear tactics.

The final point that focuses upon the lawfulness of a future legislation basing upon the Enabling Act is the most important. The Act states it in Article 5, paragraph 5 states "Moreover that, the display ceases to be effective when a different one takes over the current legislature of the Reich."

On the 29th of June of 1933 On June 29, 1933, the Dr. Hugenberg, Minister of

Agriculture and Nutrition, resigned from the office in a state of tension. Because of the time of Germany's national People's party's most prominent agent's departure this alliance was actually an idea of the Government and was not approved. This is due to the German Nationals' help had the National Socialists a majority of seats and votes. Following the demise of the alliance's accomplice Hitler's bureau Hitler secured its true persona; and, what's more was there was no chance for a new bureau to be created. The underlying reason was not unique to that as it was a part of the Enabling Act of 1923. In the Enabling Act forces have concurred to an alliance-based government that had, in all likelihood, obtained the parliamentary order. After the dissolution from German Nationals German Nationals, followed quickly by the denial of the gathering and the political nature of the bureau had, at a broad sense, altered.

In no way can it be maintained that the main forces of the protest were in the hands of the National Socialists as a whole because the presence of the German Nationals in the legislature was viewed by all parties as that voted in favor of the protest as the brake on political power. The demonstration therefore had lost its political foundation and, as a result as well as its legitimacy.

Chapter 4: Commerce And Commerce

Germany was a major influence on the disintegration of exchange and finance during the 1930s. In a state of constant deficits in the current account and fueled by an ideology that sought to consolidate power across Europe, Nazi Germany diverted its financial and foreign exchange relations into an impermanent arrangement of bilateral exchange and clearing agreements. The eyewitnesses of the present and more recent academic research has revealed that in the 1930s, Germany successfully adapted the framework to prevent financial exploitation of its exchange partners. Hirschman brought attention to Germany being the main exchange partner of the smaller European nations, and summarized this into an idea of imposition of business models in the international exchange. Then, Child investigated the common clearing framework and found that Germany did not follow these game plans to differentiate money related and actual assets from its trading partners. The discussions that were more well-established led to an international consensus that lasted for a long time.

A shrewd perspective which has recently gained acceptance was developed by Neal who recognized that the exchange terms were understood by Germany's exchange courses of action were not asymmetrical toward a German preferred positions. The evidence uncovered by Neal was in good agreement with an opportunistic view that was derived from Milward who believed that by using assets in the process of developing its financial sector in the 30s Germany gained a temporary advantage in monetary terms. Recently, Kitson contended from assessing the German foreign exchange system prior to during the conflict that Germany had to give up terms of exchange preferences to improve its political influence. This assertion has been echoed in addition from Feinstein, Temin, and Toniolo in their writing material documents of the European economy during the two wars. What they share is the absence of quantitative evidence sufficient to establish a factual assertion. The Nazi organization hid the crucial details on the mystery of the equalization of installments until 1936, only the new exchange details are available through hotspots distributed throughout the latter period of the 1930s.

The rich information base about the various segments of equalization of installments was given to the chronicles. Additionally tiny segments are included in later research. This is the duration of time that the published sources provide unidentified exchange measures. The additional component that is covered by the non-published materials includes the parts that are not included in the installment parity, like capital advancements. The parities also include the parities of foreign trade costs and receipts per nation, separated into balance-of-payments classifications as well as exchanges for the clearing account, as well as the foreign exchange trade. When you study this data, it is possible to create a detailed picture of the installment and exchange flows of Nazi Germany prior to it entered the Second World War. Analyzing these and other sources on German trade and foreign exchange strategies was not too long after that Second World War loans backing on the commitments made later to the discussions mentioned previously. The findings suggest that a foreign exchange strategy on its own is not enough to allow Germany to abuse the small. In general, the misuse appears to have begun with a single country's military control, but it was later extended to a large extent.

The Third Reich is not only an autocracy, but also an kleptocracy. Hitler's standards were not only on fascism, but as well as on burglary, loot as well as plundering. It is crucial to be aware not just because it provides a new dimension in the context of National Socialism violations but because it helps us understand the way in which The Third Reich functioned.

They were launched at the perfect moment. In 1923, Hitler ordered his stormtroopers to take over an Jewish bank in order to gain reserves. Then, in 1933, he halted the actions. However, in 1933 , they were granted free reign. The massive snatching of workers' organization premises started on the 2nd of May in 1933. Furniture and utensils, as well as beds were taken away. Attacks against Jewish temples, the demolishment of 7500 Jewish shops as well as the demolishment of many Jewish homes occurred on the alleged Reichskristallnacht 9-10 November 1938. They were also followed by the theft or the evacuation of numerous belongings of individuals as well as the property of the owners. After the Anschluss in March 1938 In March 1938, Nazis exiled Jewish residents away from their residences, and plunder the rest of their possessions; Jews were detained in the city and robbed of their fur clothes jewels, wallets, and furs.

This kind of petty stealing dwindled into insignificance when compared with the methodical taking of Jewish resources, which began swiftly after the Nazi confiscation from power during 1933. There were a variety of legitimate tools, such as department stores shops, and other businesses were targeted. Common sense The Devisenfahndungsamt of Heydrich (1936) could have brought organisations into an organization when they were in place to aid in the removal of capital of Germany and produce admissions, and created cross-examination reports. Territorial Economic Consultants' workplaces of the Nazi Party selected trustees to Jewish firmsand enacted the April 7th 1933 law to get rid of Jewish directors and owners. In the Four Year Plan utilized demanding forces. The movement was expanded following Reichskristallnacht in which the government had officially demanded an assignment, as well as Aryanization of Jewish owned or operated organisations. In the night prior to the war, there were no Jewish owned or operated organizations remained.

Around one-fifth of the purchase-outs were carried out by friends or family members with a reasonable fee or in good standing. Around 40 percent of the purchase outs were paid for the amount that was allowed by the base and that includes, for instance the term "generosity" because, according to the records there was no such thing and 40 percent were able to be constrained using coercion Gestapo and in some cases, instances, open violence. There were numerous advantages such as the fact that Regional Economic Offices of the NS received a 10% commission on the cost of Jewish organisations; and in Thuringia Thuringia, the NS Regional Economic Officer made more than a million checks similar to that and used them to buy up companies himself.

It was the backdrop for massive Jewish resources' petty robbery during the war. The activities impacted Polish property. On

September 27th 1939, Poland's German military announced a massive transfer of Polish property. They confirmed the demand on the 5th of October, 1939. On the 19th of October, 1939 Goring stated that the Four-Year Plans Office kept the entirety of Polish and Jewish properties in the domains that were consolidated. A decree was signed 17 September 1940 which created a focal entity, known as the Haupttreuhandstelle Ost, to oversee the property confiscated. in February of 1941 they comprised more than 205,000 companies ranging in size from small workshops to huge modern projects. In June 1941, fifty percent of the business sector as well as 33% of larger land-based Reich Trustees had taken over residences in the adjoining regions with no compensation. These demands, in fact were a permission for anyone Germans to plunder the resources they required. In addition, the military took the control of a large number of homesteads, in order to make sure that there was enough food for soldiers.

The German invaders also stole large quantities of social goods. In an attack against the Bernadin religious community in Radeczina in the month of November 1939 "all the precious stones and gold votives ' were "appropriated,"' as Klukowski wrote. This was only one of many incidents like this. Nation homes along the course of attack were discovered as well, and pressure was put on to their affluent owners to find out the location of secret fortunes. Soon, the process of social seizing was set on a legal base.. On the 16th of December 1939, German experts demanded the compulsory enrollment of all comparable and social belongings dating from before 1850, in addition to jewellery, instruments, coins books, furniture, and other items.

A chief of the official staff, Kajetan Muhlmann, who was recently discharged from similar obligations in Vienna was the one responsible for the entire cycle. In Nov. 1940 the enlistment was completed and Hitler's craftsman Hans Posse showed up to select the best instances for Hitler.

He was accompanied by the chiefs of the historical center for art from Germany. There was a flurry of fighting, when Hermann Goring attempted to acquire images for himself, while Hans Frank had a problem regarding the removal of prize money from his central authority. Perhaps this was not as a practical idea, however because Frank was clueless about how to display or safeguard Old Masters, and was at one time criticised by Muhlmann for hanging an art work created by Leonardo da Vinci over a radiator. Private collections were as popular as the state historical museums as well as the vast collection of art belonging to members of the Czartoryski family, which included two works by Rembrandt and Raphael, Raphael was systematically snatched away.

In the meantime, Hans Frank designed his base camp using plundered art and transportation awards that were returned to Bavaria. When American soldiers arrived at the end of 1945 they discovered the remains of a Rembrandt and an Leonardo and a 14th-century Madonna from Cracow and plundering clothes along with goblets and other items taken from Polish chapels. He even made reference to his status as a nobleman who looted. He reclaimed the bequest of the Potocki family to be used as a retreat for provincial officials and toured his property in a limousine that was big enough to draw comments from his friends, like Governor Galicia. In a bid to emulate Hitler and creating an imitation of Hitler's Berghof located in the mountains near Zakopane. He cooked up a feast of awe that led to his waist growing rapidly that he sought out an dietician as the size of his waistline was not enough for his uniform.

At the same time, normal Poles' conditions of living became increasingly worse as food resources became increasingly scarce. The petty theft and confiscation continued. Refusing toy items for social use include like the removal of equipment from colleges research facilities to be used in Germany. In fact even the Warsaw Zoo's collection of toys were not available. In the Reich itself for a time the iron and steel items such as, for example, the nursery entranceways and railings even candelabras, pots and candelabras were available to melt down and utilized in the deadly weaponry and vehicle design in Germany. In the time when winter virus began to choke in the beginning of January, 1940, the head of the clinic doctor Dr. Zygmunt Klukowski noticed, "the German police seized all coats made of sheepskin from the locals who were passing by and put only in coats.' Then, a short time later the occupation forces began to attack towns and taking all notes they found in them--similar to what happened between and after the USSR invasion in June 1942.

There was a rationale behind this. At first, Jews and Poles were considered to be sub-par. Hitler's aim was to demolish Polish culture, and then execute Polish scholars.

There was a certain belief within Nazis to believe that Jews specifically were taking things from Germans in all likelihood via 'profiteering' and misuse.' There was no evidence that Jews or Poles were incredibly refined, and they were not able to enjoy all the social status they once had. Finally this was now an everyday part of life as a financial institution in the Third Reich; thus, it was first introduced in Poland and in the USSR.

In any event there were various thinking processes, and also. The key element was the lawful extra-legal premise that fueled Hitler's power. What Hitler did and said was legal. The 'right' state grew all the way to what people often referred to as the "little Hitler's the local party supervisors, and even the grassroots members of the party. The disdain for the law was evident during the 1920s. As long as it didn't reject the essential tenets of Nazi doctrine, the extra-legal behavior was tolerated, provided it could promote the cause that of National Socialism.

Additionally The Reichstag and the official gatherings were largely quiet while the media and press were responsible for their own Propaganda Ministry, and the justice and police authorities were totally Nazified.

Everyday gatherings, people hoped for payments during the Third Reich for their sufferings during the supposed "season of war." It was an effective way to strengthen the inner unity of the group as well as forming groups within it, and establishing comfortable connections of shared dedication between pioneers and followers on every stage.

Also as the age of young Germans who were the subject of numerous dynamic Nazis could be attributed that was conceived between 1905 and 1910. It was in a conflict with financial integrity and cash and had experienced childhood during the long-winded and unreported period of conflict, and having witnessed cash decrease in value astronomically during the years of inflation from 1922 to

23. But, having gotten through the famine years, its infamous incidents of desecration and guilt, was portrayed as a god by Christopher Isherwood in his "Mr. Norris Changes Trains."

Afterward, after being in the midst of unemployment and depression beginning in 1929 It was not a big surprise to them that they were confident about holding onto what they believed was their due when the second recession hit.

In light of Jews and Poles who were robbed and degraded, this could also be the way in which the Nazis made their enemies look like they were a joke and caused them to suffer by inducing the feeling of emptiness and depriving them of their position and possessions.

When the Nazis took over an economy with a jobless rate that was nearly thirty percent. The first factor that storm troopers and other gathering people expected was a job. On July 23, 1933 Rudolf Hess guaranteed an job for anyone who was hosting a get-together beginning before the 30th of January the 30th of January, 1933. The administration in October officially set up working arrangements for people who had a number of enrollments less than 300,000 (for instance, the end of 1930) and for those from Stahlhelm, the SS, SA, and Stahlhelm who joined before the 30th of January in 1933.

In 1937, in 1937, the Reich Post Office had given more than 30,000 posts to'meriting National Socialists.' In October of 1933 they Berlin party had discovered a job for 30,000 people. Ninety percent percent of jobs that were recently available to middle-class workers within the public sector went to "old contenders.' Many were made open through exclusions as a result of the law passed on April 7th in 1933. A lot of Nazis held positions before but, in reality, they employed this strategy to increase their standing. The duration of enrollment in the group was counted in computing status which meant there were greater opportunities for advancement. Usually, the posts were not as essential. A study of Hamburg Sickness Fund in 1934 found that it employed 228 directors, which was more directors than was actually needed. Nearby railroad frameworks employed more than 1,000 new employees in 1933 and 1934. In general, new workers were judged insufficient for the positions they were delegated. A number of workers nearly accepted the money without even going to work.

Theft has been repeated. Friedrich Stabel, the new director of the public understudies' union from Sept. 1933, bought cars and clothes with reserve funds from the association, and even employed a band to provide his entertainment. The crowd was drawn by parties, and there were many new ones in the years from 1933, when attendance grew into the thousands following the seizing of power. From the 1st of January 1934 to December 31 of the year 1941 saw more than 11,000 court cases for the misappropriation of reserves for gathering.

However, in many areas in the Nazi forces, debasement of contraptions continued unchecked. The most well-known were The Labor Front. It was an incredible organization that covered entirely employed individuals, and supplanting Trade Unions, with an massive number of employees and all former worker's guild property, and a variety of commercial activities. Its development department was governed through Anton Karl, who had sentiments for theft and robbery that began in the 1920s. Karl offered more than 580,000 Reichsmarks in rewards in 1936-7 in order to ensure agreements. Karl offered endowments to anyone who he considered to be significant. For instance, the first person to be Hitler's protectors received silk shirts, chasing guns and a trip to Italy for his wife. The Labor Front also rewarded Karl by granting him permission to build a new sleeping area in Berlin. In 1935, the Labor Front gave Hitler's auxiliaries in the same way as his picture photographer, 20,000 imprints for Christmas gifts. A spy who was revealing the imprints to the restricted SPD observed, the defilement within this section of the Labor Front is tremendous, and the general norm of ethics is likewise very low.'

It was particularly relevant to Labor Front's founder Robert Ley, whose compensation for this job, 4,040 Reichsmarks per year and was increased to 22,000 Reichsmarks in the role of Reich Organization Leader of the Party and 700 RM as an Reichstag representative as well as 400 RM as an Prussian State Councilor. In the beginning, the Labor Front put in mass requests for his books as well as handouts. He earned the equivalent of 50,000 RM per year by altering the newspaper he edited. The costs of his diversion were covered by Labor Front. Labor Front, which additionally allowed him to keep his home in Berlin's lux Grunewald location until 1938. He travelled on a journey that was planned through the Labor Front, the travel department for culture and industry that was known as Strength Through Joy, on another vessel named, invariably The Robert Ley. The group was comprised of several blue-eyed and blonde young women for "friendship," and was flanked by two mariners every when he arrived on the ready to ensure that his safety and not fall off the boat.

Others Nazi pioneers were also not too far from Ley in constructing themselves with their nests. Hermann Goringburn burned through 15 million RM for the repair of his lodge, and another 500 000 RM of the money of the citizens for maintenance regularly. He also owned six lodges, chateaus, an Alpine chalet as well as one estate located in Berlin and a private trainthat had the capacity of ten cars as well as a bakery that was working to satisfy his desire to eat cream-based cakes. The taxpayer spent an additional 1.32 million RM to upgrade the train, even with extravagant decorations and fittings.

To ensure that the taxman would not examine Goring as well as others Nazi pioneers' efforts in 1939, the legislature decided 1939 that it was their responsibility to examine workplaces located in Berlin or Munich and Munich, in conjunction with Nazi authorities that might decide not to look for any contradictions.

There were many famous jokes concerning Nazi debasement. Traditionalists are 'people who is compensated generously for an task that an Nazi enjoys their appearance.' Two Nazi officials are walking along the streets when one them spots a note with a 50-Reichsmark and takes it. "I will donate it to the party's Winter Aid program," the man says. "Why take it the long approach?" his friend replies"It's simple - "simply put it in the right direction in pockets." It was the cabaret. Wilhelm Finck was sent to an execution camp for having a sly joke in 1934. At the time, he continued to sit on the stage at Berlin's Catacomb club, his arm raised in the Nazi salute, and the tailor was estimating him to wear a different outfit. "What type of jacket do I need?" Finck asked the tailor. "With pockets completely open, according to the latest fashion," Finck answered.

One driving Nazi however, was exempted from the general discontent regarding this kind of thing. Hitler himself was a fan of fame for integrity, perhaps even Puritanism. He was unmarried, a vegetarian smoker, non-drinker, and non-smoker He portrayed a scene of his private joy in Germany. Another joke involved the children from Joseph Goebbels, the Propaganda Minister, escorting tea at the residences of Goring, Ley, and other driving Party figures. After every visit, they would return to their homes raving about the desserts, cakes and various sweets.

After a trip to Hitler however the place where they buy malt espresso as well as some small plain rolls. They inquire with their father: "Isn't a Fuhrer an member of the Party at this point?"

Hitler made his morally correct image by denying his pay during his time as Reich as Chancellor. It amounted up to 45,000 Reichsmarks annually as well as his annual costs stipendof an additional 18,000. In the public's view, he was not informed that he had never settled any debt, nor that he was never able to settle any tax, nor in 1934, when his Munich charge office tried to slap a charge of 400,000 Reichsmarks upon him having fallen behind in his financial obligations during 1934. The inscrutable authorities received a peaceful inspection from Gestapo who then rejected the whole issue and smashed Hitler's duty papers to make the deal. In the end, a grateful Hitler offered the director of the Munich charge office a tax-free annual compensation increase of 2,000 Reichsmarks to support his time in office.

The actual pay of Hitler was derived from the sale that included Mein Kampf, mass purchased by Nazi Party associations, and totaling 1.2 million Reichsmarks only in

1933. From 1937 Hitler earned huge sums from the copyright fees imposed for his image on postage stamps (50 million Reichsmarks within one year) costs and sovereignties for each printing of his addresses on the press.

The legacy that were left to him by his donation to the Adolf Hitler Donation of German Industry as well as after Hindenburg's death in 1934 from the President's assets, which were later excluded from the normal method of evaluating. He was able to establish an official subsidize for his departure that, in 1942, had reached an astonishing total of 24 million impressions.

Hitler used this method to provide annuities to old extremists and averse to Semitic scholars whom he described as Nazi "antecedents," and in the meantime, to over 100 Nazi activists. They had been imprisoned in the Weimar Republic, and afterward was offered at the request of the military contaminating its commanders in order in order to convince them to accept any action that was that was against their system. He provided them with artistic works of the military for the camp of the regimental He also paid 100,000 Reichsmarks annually for officials to be on'rest fixes', he widened the annuities of officials who had resigned and provided Field Marshal von Mackensen an exempt tax-exempt bequest to land along with 350,000 Reichsmarks to cover cost of designing. Then he repeated the same signal to other blue-blooded landowners who were waiting for the return to the Kaiser. The generous nature of Hitler's generosity proved to be much more generous during the war. He he granted commanders blessings in the form of money, art works properties, works of art, and much more. At the same time, speedy progress, the creation of new commanders and Field Marshals were rewarded with the rapidly increasing pay scales. Hitler introduced massive month-to- monthly increases to the salaries of clergymen and other authorities He also gave his favorite stoneworker Arno Breker a quarter of one million Reichsmarks as a gift in 1940. He also, as usual, he spread his gifts among vast parts from the clergy, military, share assistance and social elites. The result was that one of the major and often ignored factors that held the top level within the Nazi Party together was defilement which was the receiving of massive blessings, huge increases in wages, and properties. This strengthened the relationship that they enjoyed with Hitler in an alliance of patronage which, in the end it was repeated to a lesser extent through the command chain up to base.

In the course of during the conflict, growth of defilement was accompanied by an increase in the size and strength of looting plundering, theft, and plundering as has been discussed on the account of Poland. This was not true in countries like France, Denmark, or Italy.

Hitler and Goring were not in doubt of securing artworks to their collections, particularly for Hitler's planned workshop exhibition hall, which was located in his neighborhood of Linz with important collections that were there, as well when everyday life was destroyed in towns with a lot of activity.

German officials and supervisors were frequently ready to eat up art pieces at reduced prices from desperate Belgians or Dutchmen looking for money to keep them from starving.

The extermination of Europe's Jews began in the second quarter of 1941. It resulted in the transfer of Jewish sources under control of the Nazis either through the transfer of their property and organizations, or the taking from their bodies. The major German banks gained in particular from the removal of gold fillings out of the teeth of the dead Jews. All of this was further added to a sense of guilt for wrongdoing, which was a further factor that held the Nazi forces together , even as the military situation was weakened.

Plundering and looting also were more of a task to complete, however. In recent times the extremist German Antiquarian Gotz Aly has contended that it was so broad the point that maintained the majority of traditional Germans committed to the system throughout the war by keeping their expectations of everyday conveniences to a reasonable level. The authorities and the fighters returned normal parcels of food items and shoes, clothing and much more to their families back home. Aly is a reference to letters from the wartime writer Heinrich Boll that went with these bundles, which included margarine and cheddar as well as other food items that could be purchased economically in France however were very difficult to get in Germany. The food, clothes furniture, and other things that were not found in an area for exiled Jews were all taken over and shipped back to Germany effectively. In the beginning of the period of three months in 1943 for instance, troops of the 18th armed forces at Leningrad's front Leningrad front sent more than 3,000,000 boxes back to their homes packed with items that varied in nature, definitely more than what was sent the other way, despite the many hardships German soldiers endured during wintertime Russian winter. There was a raging exchange of stolen hides for example.

To a greater extent, German companies demanded, acquired, or almost taken control of primary resources from nations that had been defeated to boost the economy at home. They ranged from the constrained taking over of adversaries Western European firms by the synthetics giant I G Farben to the purchase over 8,000 railroad vehicles from Belgian railways through the company's German partner. Gotz Aly said that this allowed German war-related ventures to go forward and empowered the German state to carry on the charges.

Defilement could influence the way in which this Nazi party and the military assembly. But the belief system was also important here but perhaps even more than. Although Nazi heads were fond of the tangible benefits and characteristics of power, they never were less influenced by that authority regardless of their philosophical views. Perhaps, the most important thing is that it was the philosophy of thought rather than the necessity or desire for plunder, that drove the Nazi policy of removing Europe's Jews. It's true that the Nazis made a number of options to not waste funds, based on their perceptions that were focused on taking care of and preserving four million Soviet detainees from war they rounded up in 1941 and 1942 as well as the millions of Jews they enslaved in Poland and in the Ukraine in the Ukraine and Belarus. Whatever the case the primary decision to execute the individuals involved was not a result of money, but rather of a faith system: of Nazis dislike of the people they considered to be Slavic subhumans, and even more so and firmly, of their determination to rid Europe and perhaps finally an entire universe from the significant Jewish threat to Germany's existence.

Despite the immense work that has been done in the last few years, we know little about the effects of looting and plundering in the German economy, particularly during the conflict.

However whatever they were the plundering itself was of a sufficient size to continue to plague us over sixty years later and the ongoing compensatory activities for social goods and various kinds of property proves repeatedly. Perhaps at last it is also true that the effects of debasement upon the Third Reich and how it performed, both in the both at home and abroad, was one of the rare examples of the negative effects of unlimited force in general. But, it's an old fashioned statement and there is no appropriate way to end this short speech than to quote Lord Acton the Regius Professor in Modern History: "Force will generally degenerate and force in its totality undermines."

Chapter 5: The Jewish Question

In the archive of human atrocities in the archives of human atrocities, the Germans' inhumane treatment of Jews during Nazi Germany are among the most horrific remembered. The Holocaust is so distinct because it was widely documented. Through films and meticulous documents, we've been witness to the Germans with their precise mass murder and their complete denial of their empathy. Concerning the shameful mark that was left over western development there can be no question. Yet, a few issues remain. What made that the Nazi party so attractive to the German population? Are the citizens of Germany attracted by Hitler's incomprehensible appeal, or were they captivated by the constant propaganda of the Nazis or did they think they were merely doing what they wanted to do? Was it due to a source of this lust prompted this kind of fervor?

The Nazi Party was appealing too quickly to the German populace in the years following Hitler and his group offered a solution to almost every issue that confronted the population. For instance the Party program tended to focus on the loss of German troops of WWI. The Nazis made use of the popular belief that Germany's military had been "betrayed" to the Weimar Republic's first legislators. In this way, they persuaded German citizens to believe that the defeat in the War with Democracy.

Another major goal that was pursued by The Nazis was to revoke the Treaty of Versailles. This agreement, signed by the Allies after the German defeat during WWI was designed to degrade Germany. Germany had to end its military aid, neutralize its land located on the left bank the Rhine River as well as pay an incredibly high amount of reparations, give up its provinces, and accept full accountability for the war's beginning. This arrangement was highly unpopular to Germans. There was no official from the government that could support the arrangement. But it was the Nazi development used it as an invigorating factor. Here's an excerpt from the flyer that proclaimed an Hitler speech:

Adolf Hitler stands up. Join us in voicing your displeasure against Germany having to bear the war to blame. Oppose and against the Peace Treaty of Versailles, which was forced upon us by the only responsible party that is the Jewish global statehouse of the stock market. For every German dismantling the agreement will bring feelings of awe and strength. The Nazi party provided a solution to accomplish this.

In many of his speeches as he rose to the presidency, Hitler regularly talked about the "treacherous" attitude in the Weimar government and its methods to fulfill the terms of the agreement. On the 24th of February 1920, at the first assembly of public members for the German Worker's Party (later to be renamed NSDAP), Hitler delineated the agenda for the gathering. The principal point was the notion of a bind together Germany with the ball "assurance." The following paragraph spoke sincerely about the Paris Treaty: "We request uniformity in rights for the German citizens in their interactions with other nations, and the cancellation of Peace Treaties of Versailles and St. Germain." So, the Nazis took up a place that could give the German people a chance to restore their nationalist pride and remove the sword off the back of the military. In the absence of this agreement, Germany could revamp its military, which had always played a major role in its character.

Another reason why another reason why the Nazis appealed to the German populace was the staggering financial hardships that followed WWI. The high inflation of 1923 made it necessary for home owners to use ineffective German money to light flames. With each turbulence in the economy, the development of Nazi participation decreased.

The economy was in decline, Nazi enlistment grew. The advance leap made by the Nazis in 1932 was due to the 1929 devastation which spread throughout the world.

The crazed desire to be needed of the time created difficulties in the networks of rural ranchers. The majority of town life was a network of and individuals who helped each other. But, the more difficult it was to utilize cash, the further networks began to break apart. Public Socialism was able to attract these splintering networks through land, blood and ideas about public unity.

An attractive attribute from the Nazi Party to Germany's bourgeois and the top of its list was its rejection of Marxism. in the 30s, a frenetic urban common was beginning to unite with those of German Communist as well as Socialist coalitions. It was a serious threat to the center and the upper society. Hitler had a more ferocious advancement, which was more sorted out, and more radical than the most to the left

Reichstag. The bourgeois and upper classes did not require the same kind of revolution as Russia. A state that was extremist would need its own installment, but it would not demand for the redistribution and distribution of all private property.

The Nazis communicated with the Germans through fueling the known patterns of hostility towards Semitism. The history of anti-Semitism can be found throughout Germany. One of the sources that Nazi development relied on was paranoid fears based on a book called "Conventions of the Elders of Zion." This document was first published in the latter half in the early 1800s. It portrayed a rumored global plan to rule and govern the entire world. In accordance with Protocols that were signed, the Jews intended to employ a variety of weapons, such as invoking an image of the French Revolution, progressivism, socialism, communism, and political agitation in order to undermine European cultural.

According to experts in history in The Encyclopedia of the Holocaust, the account was said to be crafted in the midst of the Dreyfus Affair (1894) by Pyotr Ivanovich Rachkovskiwho was the head of a different section in the Russian secret police in Paris. The French Right required a document to entrap Richard Dreyfus in the supposed cooperation. The Czar continued to use the protocol to assist his opponent who was a part of Semitic agreements in Russia. Then the Protocol made its way to Germany. In 1919 and 1923 Alfred Rosenburg, a Nazi ideologist, wrote five widely circulated leaflets on the connivance. In addition, Julius Streicher's essay, Der Strummer (the aggressor) is often referred to conventions.

In his argument, Hitler accepted that because Jewish pioneers had ensured that the Protocols were in fact implemented, they ought to be in effect at the time. Hitler also boasted that he had learned a lot from the Protocols concerning political interests concealment, redirection and other association strategies. Alfred Rosenburg constructed many ways to think about acknowledging that the "reality" in the Protocols. These thoughts drew many Germans as well as other Europeans to join The Nazi party.

Julius Streicher was a Nazi advocate who chose to make a career to thwart the advancing adversaries of Semitism. He denigrated Jews with abrasive and inhumane ways in his famous paper Der Strummer for a long period of. Here's one of the many instances of Streicher's disdain for Jews:

The head of the family purges some drops of fresh or powdered blood, then saturates the fingers of the left hand it, and then splashes, adorns by it, all the food items placed on the tables. At this point the head of the family states"We ask that God give the 10 diseases to all enemies of the Jewish faith.' They then take a meal. Additionally, towards the end the family's head declares: 'May all the

Gentiles perish, like the kid's blood was contained in the wine and bread.'

Der Strummer was a broadly read weekly newspaper. The most notable feature was the first-page children's shows, which featured Jews to be vampires or as attackers.

It had a huge impact on German general sentiments against Jews. Streicher also wrote and published an children's book that taught children to hate Jews from the very beginning.

Another strategy for capturing what was in the German mind was to think of an unadulterated race , homogenous hereditary populaces. The Nazis expanded the Aryan norms, which promoted the idea of pride in being of German blood. The significance that was associated with being German was growing since they were viewed as the dominant mental race really. They were typically more gifted than other races in terms of quality too. In addition, the fact that the German residents being viewed as superior to be a success, they were advised that through their work, even if they were males, and also by their success and vigor, the German population could create an appealing society even if they were women. After having experienced the pessimism which was the general mental state in the 1920s simple and simplified ideas were attractive.

It was the Nazi Party consolidated the issues of the German government's sale out during WWI as well as the establishment of Versailles as well as the Weimar republic's lack of prudence in taking responsibility for its economy, the public's solidarity, fear of Marxism as well as anti-Semitism and the German people's ethnicity into a stunning proclamation bundle. The main purpose was to shoot at the German public's fears and expectation until the Nazi beliefs captivated them. Hitler's greatest virtuoso demonstrated his ability to use publicity as a surgeon's tool. He knew how to focus on specific groups and make them feel arousing on emotions. Since the vast majority of them were ignorant and uninformed, this was where the man made his most memorable efforts. In Mein Kampf that with the aim of having promulgation successful, it should be done be academically based. the lowest level: "the more prominent the audience it's proposed to reach and the more educated the level must remain... it is best to avoid excessive scholarly demands on our citizens... " This is where is how Hitler's psyche worked. He aimed his attention at the biggest possible crowd and crafted his promulgation stage and running track for the smallest common element of knowledge. In this way, he enticed crowds and was able to determine the overall outcome.

In 1941, following the Soviet Union's German invasion In 1941, during the German invasion of the USSR, the Nazis began their task of killing with vigor.

Nazi commandos were testing various strategies to be executed as a large crowd within the line. They anticipated that shooting people would cause a lot of distress for their staff, so they began they were thinking of more effective ways to kill.

Exploratory gas trucks killed mentally disabled people in Poland from 1939 onwards. The harmful exhaust was siphoned into a closed compartment that would imprison those in the.

Nazis assembled in January 1942 during the Wannsee Conference to arrange what they called an "last solution to"the Jewish inquiry" which was to slaughter the entire European Jewish population, 11 million people, through the elimination of Jews and the constrained work.

What exactly was Auschwitz?

Auschwitz was at first the name of a Polish sleeper cell for armed forces in the southern part of Poland. Nazi Germany attacked and invaded Poland in September 1939 and, by May 1940, it had transformed Auschwitz into a detention facility for political prisoners.

With the infamous untruth "Arbeit Macht Frei', which is a passageway in German the zone signifies that work is liberated - it later became called Auschwitz I.

But, as war and Holocaust intensified as the war dragged on, the Nazi system was able to significantly expand the area.

The first people to be gassed were members of a group from Polish as well as Soviet prisoners in September of 1941. The work began on a different camp Auschwitz II-Birkenau the following month. It became a massive gas chambers, where more than thousand people were killed up to November 1944. In addition, the crematoria was where their bodies were burnt.

German synthetic chemical company I.G. Farben built and operated in an engineering elastic manufacturing facility in Auschwitz III-Monolith. Other privately-owned companies like Krupp and Siemens-

Schuckert also had factories that employed prisoners as slaves. In both cases, Primo Levi, as well as Nobel Prize victor Elie Wiesel suffered through the brutal confinement of Monowitz.

When Auschwitz was taken prisoner, the camp was home to over 40 camps as well as subcamps.

What was the process that made Auschwitz operate?

From all over, Europeans were packed into railway cars with no toilets, windows seats, food, or even seats and then moved to Auschwitz.

The group that was last asked to strip exposed, and then gave the boot to "delousing" doublespeak, which was used to refer to those gas rooms.

Gatekeepers from the alleged "Sterile Institute" dropped Zyklon B gas pellets that broke the ground into fixed loads and believe that the people will pass away. It took about 20 minutes. The thick dividers were unable to conceal the screams of the suffering inside.

Then Sonderkommandos - detainees of various kinds generally, Jews compelled to work for gatekeepers or be executed - would take off fake glasses, appendages hair, teeth, and other items prior to transporting the bodies to incinerators. The bodies' remains were covered with manure.

The Final Solution

The source to the "Last solution," the Nazi plan to eliminate the Jewish public, is still unclear. The only thing that is certain is that the eradication of Jews was the culmination of the Nazi strategy, executed under the direction set by Adolf Hitler. "Last Solution "Last Option" was realized in phases.

Following the time that after the Nazi Party took control, discrimination imposed by the state led to the threat of Jewish the enactment of blacklists, enactment, "Aryanization," and the "Evening of

Broken Glass" massacre that all aimed to remove Jews from German cultural. Following World War II, anti-Jewish strategy grew into a comprehensive plan to think, and eventually eliminate European Jewry.

The Nazis established ghettos and invaded Poland. Western and clean European Jews were in front of these Ghettos. In the course of Germany's invasion of the Soviet Union in 1941, the mobile murdering teams (Einsatzgruppen) began to slaughter the entire Jewish population. The methods employed, primarily gas vans or shooting was soon seen as ineffective, and also as an emotional burden to the executed.

Following the Wannsee Conference in January 1942 The Nazis began the exact elimination of Jews from all over Europe to six camps of elimination established in the previous Polish area : Chelmno, Belzec, Sobibor, Treblinka, Auschwitz-Birkenau, and Majdanek. Elimination camps were a focus for murder designed to completely decimate. About 3 million Jews were gassed in the annihilation camps.

In the end it was the "Last solution" (View this term from the glossary) consisted of gassings shootings, and arbitrary displays of sickness, fear, and hunger that symbolized the death of about 6 million Jews, which is a total of 66% of Europe's Jewish people.

Important Dates

June 22, 1941:

Murdering squads are part of the German invasion of and the Soviet Union. German flexible execution teams are referred to as exceptional obligation units (Einsatzgruppen) are assigned to massacre Jews in the course of the invasion of in the Soviet Union. They follow the German armoured force when it moves across the Soviet region, and then commit mass murder. At first the diverse executing crews shoot Jewish men primarily. Soon, wherever they go, they kill all Jewish man or woman and even a youngster with no regard for gender or age. By the time 1943 dawns the portable executing squads will have killed more than one million Jews as well as a multitude of sectarians, Roma (Gypsies) as well as Soviet the political leaders.

December 8 in 1941:

The first community to execute gets started. The Chelmno focused on execution begins activities. The Nazis later built up to five camps in the same manner: Belzec, Sobibor, Treblinka Auschwitz-Birkenau (part of the Auschwitz complex) and Majdanek. In Chelmno victims are confined to the gas vans (airtight fixed trucks fitted with motor fumes which are pumped to interior compartments). There are three camps: Belzec, Sobibor, and Treblinka camps utilize carbon monoxide gas generated by fixed motors that are joined with gas chambers. Auschwitz-Birkenau is the most infamous of the murder camps is home to four massive gas chambers using Zyklon B (View This Term in the Glossary) (glasslike hydrogen cyanide) performing specialist. The gas chambers in Majdanek make use of carbon monoxide and Zyklon B. (View this word from the Glossary) A large number of Jews are executed in gas chambers of the murder camps as an important element in the "Last Solutions."

January 20th 1942:

Wannsee Conference and the "Last Solution". It is the Wannsee Conference, a gathering between the SS (the top guards in the Nazi state) and German government offices, begins in Berlin. They discuss and aid in the implementation of the "Last Solution," which is now being implemented. In Wannsee it is it is believed that the S.S. assesses that the "Last Solution" (View This word on the Glossary) will encompass eleven millions of European Jews, including those from countries that are not occupied, such as Ireland, Sweden, Turkey as well as Great Britain. Between the autumn between 1941 and 1944 the German railways transported a lot of people to the grave in execution concentration camps in Poland. Poland.

With the constant rise of the problematic way to speak in both America and Europe, it is essential to remember that when speaking in the U.S. and Europe, it is crucial to consider the way that disregarding different voices can cause moral decay within a society. As an example, a few middle Jewish characteristics are applicable to medicine and medical care, focusing on the preservation of life. The German professional clinical network had evicted Jews from their jobs through workplace segregation, and blame, a step ahead of important Nazi laws. Professional hospitals renounced their obligations to the patient as an individual in order to promote a focus on money and hygiene. These in the last few years, when grants were announced, was incorporated into professional morals-based education programs for German students in clinical studies. The obsession with racial-public character morality grew into a mostly destructive type of clinical destruction. Although the speed of change was due to the presence of a myriad of complexities beyond the scope of a single research paper, the ethnocentric disdain for voices from competent organizations also contributed to the debasement of social norms. We believe that this method of separation was not only an element in the emergence of the use of Jews specifically, but it also served as a way of delaying social lessons that could have thwarted the traps of a skilled society that were a part of Nazi need more in and in the vast majority of cases.

We have to balance Jewish lessons by recording an examination of Third Reich medication, specifically the advancement of the T-4 killing system in a philosophical and contextual study in various lessons. The recorded model outlines how the medical calling may not serve its clients and can create smaller gatherings but only to a small extent, depending on how much the organization has decided to include those voices that are being snubbed inside itself as a way to examine itself. The model will focus on six fundamental Jewish characteristics--life, harmony with equity, fairness and grant as well as genuineness of goal--that might have inspired medical professionals to protect minorities had these principles not been obliterated or ignored by the people who created the Third Reich medication. These principles are based upon their roots in the Jewish category from the Written as well as Oral Torah, just as later, more compelling Jewish writings tend to specifically define doctors as experts. These lessons repeatedly highlight the inherent expert responsibility of physicians towards their patients to make decisions about their wellbeing, existence and finally the possibility of the possibility of passing. These truly erroneous mistakes and the terrible disappointments of the Third Reich depend on this primary severing of the doctor-patient relationship, as well as the degrading of the clinically-focused skills demonstrated by patients.

Advanced medical professionals may not realize the wide-ranging role that doctors performed in the era of cultural acceleration and destruction during the Third Reich. While the Nuremberg doctors' trial was a catalyst for understanding some of the most egregious actions, (pp17-18), the medicalization and the sanitization of sterilization and destructive practices required the assistance of the network of clinical experts.

Chapter 6: Second World War

The year 1939 was the most populous. There were approximately 2 billion people living on this globe. The most accurate estimates show that somewhere between of 62 to 78 million of them would die because of WWII, which is more than three percent of the population. While previous wars resulted in the deaths of civilians Five regular citizens were particularly affected by WWII and a large percentage of WWII European losses being experienced by regular people. Between 9.8 or 10.4 million ordinary citizens were killed due to motives of race or politics by Nazism Nazi system (Auerbach 1992). The war-related deaths were not uniform across nations regardless of whether they were military deaths due to battle, normal passes of citizens, or the Holocaust which was the division of 1939's population who died in a huge display of nations influenced by the war. Within European nation states, Germany and Poland endured the most severe losses. For similar reasons, American causalities in the

European and Asian theaters combined were over 400,000, the majority of which were officers. Likewise, there were death tolls were all-encompassing were reported in the U.K.

The majority of men died in the conflict, resulting in lower male/female ratios in Europe following the war, similar to many dads were absent in the participants' teen period. The male tendency in deaths was concentrated among troopers, the figures for an ordinary citizen, and the holocaust deaths were, to a large extent unaffected. With 3 million deaths in the military the most affected country as per our records was Germany.

One immediate result of war between nations and periods was the plight of those who were missing their father at the age of at the age of ten. The most severe effects occurred in the war-ravaged nations of Austria, Germany, and Poland. For Austria and Germany approximately four out of four children were without their fathers at the age of 10 in the course of the conflict. After that war, their legacy persists as a lot of men from 1950-1955 had fathers that died. In Germany there was a mere 33% of people aged 10 or older in the period did not live with their biological father. Rates of missing dads fall dramatically across the globe after the war. There are war-related spikes that occur across different countries (Italy, France, Denmark and Belgium) but the differences between the pre- and post-war times isn't as emotional.

One way in which WWII could have affected grown-up health and SES outcomes is the issue of hunger. World War II caused a several severe food-related emergencies that led to a variety of difficulties and might have had long-term effects on survivors' health. In particular, prior to the beginning in the German occupation of Poland the condition of the non-Germans was blemished. The average caloric intake for the Polish population was 930 calories by 1941. The situation was particularly horrendous at Warsaw Ghetto. Warsaw Ghetto, where normal portions of food were approximately 186 calories per day during 1941.

In the winter and fall of 1941-1994, Greece was struck by extreme starvation, resulting in up to 200,000 people dying (Hionidou 2006). Then, during WWII, Greece was under Bulgarian, German, and Italian occupation. The suffering was, for most of the time caused through three elements:

1. Occupiers demanded a ban on maritime travel.

2. The costs for ranchers were so low that they weren't ready to market their products.

3. There was a lot of diversity between the various areas of the country that was diminished by occupation.

The good life situation returned to acceptable levels by the close of 1942. Neelson as well as Stratman (2011) make use of Cohort Data to demonstrate that children who were malnourished aged 1 to 2 years old at the time was a significantly lower risk.

The combination of a barricade for food and an extremely cold winter led to an extreme hunger emergency in 1944/1945, across the Netherlands. More than 20,000 deaths, mainly for older people, can be due to the starvation. The outbreak of hunger came to an end when the German occupation in May 1945. A generally favored population was a major factor in the Dutch hunger at a calm period and in a small in a quiet area. Patients who were starved during pregnancy are found to be afflicted by the adverse effects of mental and emotional problems, as well as fixation as well as diabetes and coronary illnesses, and suffer more from the anthropometric and financial indicators.

Germany was hit by hunger between 1945 and 1948 after the food supply from the occupied countries was stopped. Within the U.S. occupation zone, the Office of Military Government for Germany set a goal of 1550 calories per day during 1945. In the most long periods of occupation, the goal could never be accomplished. In some areas, the regular daily calories were about 700 calories (Gimbel and 1968). Death rates increased by a factor of 4 for adults and 10 for children in this time. With a good collection of cash and a change during June 1948 nutrition deficiency was averted (Zink 1997).

The time of World War II in Europe, Germany looked to maintain an eminent separation from wars that lasted for a long time. The strategy of Germany was to beat its adversaries through a series of small-scale missions. Germany quickly dominated some in Europe and was able to do so for more than two years using a different strategy for military known as"the "Raid" (also known as "Blitzkrieg" (lightning conflict). The rapid assault strategy required the centralization of weapons used by enemies (tanks as well as planes and ordnance) on a limited front. This would cause the enemy to breach their safeguards which allowed tanks with armored armour to move quickly and roam in unison behind enemy lines, causing a flurry of stun and confusion for the enemy's security measures. German airpower prevented the opponent from having enough resupplying or redeploying their power and thus sending fortifications that would close gaps on the sides.

Germany wins (1939/1942)

* Poland (assaulted in September 1939)

* Denmark (April 1940)

* Norway (April 1940)

* Belgium (May 1940)

* Netherlands (May 1940)

* Luxembourg (May 1940)

* France (May 1940)

* Yugoslavia (April 1941)

* Greece (April 1941)

Germany was not defeated by Great Britain, which was protected from German attacks through the English Channel, Royal Navy and Royal Air Force (Raf)

On June 22nd, 1941 German powerhouses appeared out of thin air and began to attack at the Soviet Union. But, Germany was unable to defeat its Soviet Union, which along with Great Britain and the United States defeated the war and defeated Germany in May 1945.

Despite the ongoing war against Great Britain, German powers began to attack in the Soviet Union in June 1941. From the beginning the German Blitzkrieg seemed to be successful. Soviet power was pushed back by more than 600 miles the door of Moscow and suffered a lot of mishaps. Then, in December of 1941 Hitler unpredictably declared war against

America. United States, which therefore included the enormous military and financial capabilities towards the alliance that was shown against it. Another German attack on the Soviet Union in 1942 reached the shores of the Volga River and the city of Stalingrad. However the Soviet Union dispatched a counteroffensive in November 1942, which ended up capturing and killing a complete German army at Stalingrad.

Germany was unable to defeat its adversaries in the Soviet Union, which, together and Great Britain and the United States had averted Germany's actions. Germany was caught up in a lengthy war, which eventually led to its defeat in the month of May 1945.

Raid strategies had undoubtedly significant influence in the crushing of Germany's adversaries. The Germans certainly had a dominant air power through the Ju-87 Stuka jump aircraft. The Luftwaffe controlled the skies, with a bigger number of aircraft and also a stronger aircraft. In the field, in every instance it was a completely distinct issue. In the air, British tanks as well as French tanks were a lot bigger than the Panzers (German tanks). This made them unrivaled. They British and French were able to spread their tanks across the country. They provided every infantry unit the same amount of tanks. Perhaps a few, perhaps several more, but the underlying message was they were very autonomous and were battled in close proximity to infantry. The difference with German tanks was the fact that they were moved into divisions. They had heavily armored Panzer divisions with about 300 to 400 tanks, which were significantly superior to an infantry zone with just only a few tanks. The massive tanks were part of Blitzkrieg which helped greatly. The subject of shock took on an important role in the conflict. Poland was home to a large amount of soldiers, and if they had realized that the Germans were on the way, Germany actually would have been victorious, but they would have suffered larger losses.

The Raid was an excellent military strategy, however it wasn't the main motive behind how Germany was able to defeat its adversaries. Furthermore, Germany was thoughtfully new to the idea of attacking and was aware of areas where it would not be required to enter.

The Maginot Line was a progression of powerful powers across the German-French border. It ran approximately 93 miles long and yet was only 250 miles from the ocean. The French began to build expansions, however, they were unable to complete the task on time. The French were home to 400,000 soldiers along their Maginot Line, and both the French as well as the Germans knew that assaulting this Maginot Line would prove destructive to the entire Maginot Line. The Allies believed that the Germans were likely to attack through northern Belgium. They believed that this was due to the fact that southern Belgium is home to the Ardennes an area of sloping covered in forest. The Allies believed that they would be attacked by Germans were going to attack from this point if and an important IF in that moment, would last for 14 days.

To get through the thick forests and everything done in small quantities. The Germans attacked from this point and the French were left with just 100,000 inexperienced, unequipped soldiers. The Germans made it through the mountains in just 3 days, and then through other areas by thousands. 1800 Panzers made it through and infantry units made it through in a jillions.

They were in France and captured those Allied troops in Belgium. The way they were able to overcome within three days was that they had accomplished a huge task. The end result could be unique as 500 000 soldiers from the north might return to aid in the event that it took longer. The speed of progress was due to the efforts of German military street builders, architects and demolition teams. They destroyed trees, laid streets, and cleared the course for the Germans to advance. This was a different strategy different from Blitzkrieg to allow the Germans to eliminate their enemies. Hitler's virtuosity and skill made a huge difference. He used his army's first flood to hover and entrap the 500,000 of his allied soldiers in Belgium. The initial wave brought them as the rest of German soldiers were advancing on France. They covered 200 miles in 7 days, and shortly, 12,000,000 exiles were infesting France's roads. The Luftwaffe took arbitrary shots at the exiles' deaths, however it was not wise. The way in which the French military and government leaders were reorganized in the past did not assist. The Chief of Staff was Gamelin.

He was clever; however the man was not brave. In addition, he was 62. He was not a frequent visitor to his French central command in Vincennes (which was not equipped with any radio interconnections, which did make the situation better). He was quite older than the position. The Premier was snubbed to account by

Marshal Petain, who was at 83. Holland was attacked and decimated. They surrendered on May 14 and Belgium abandoned the following day on the 27th of May. The 25th of May Bologne collapsed, the 26th of Calais. Hitler had prevailed. Dunkirk was defeated on June 4 and the Allies returned with a smashed and wounded. The English captured any boats they could locate and brought ships to help clear the soldiers. Hitler described the battle that took place in Dunkirk to be one of his most significant German victories ever. Germans were celebrating the night of Dunkirk.

Mussolini was a war veteran who became Hitler's ally on June 10. Mussolini was quite useful to Hitler since he controlled a portion parts of Northern Africa and Greece under his control. However the Allies entered and swept through the Italian powers extremely quickly. Hitler was quick to come to his Italian allies' assistance and took the Allies away with paratroopers (the first time they were actually used). Hitler was able to take over the country within a few weeks. He didn't have even any concept of what was happening when he took over the land, but his decision to assist Mussolini proved fatal towards his primary goal which was to conquer Russia. If he had stepped in on Russia within a half-month prior (how was it that long to help Mussolini) at the time it is believed today that it could have been possible that he had defeated Russia. It wasn't the Russian military that decimated the Germans. The cause was Russian winter. Hitler's takeover of his foes was not the direct result of Blitzkrieg (even even though it performed an important role) however, it was because of Hitler's ability.

He convinced Germans to crush their enemies through discourse. He was known as an exceptional speaker. In the end, sadly for the fighting, was an incredibly brilliant. He could strategically place his troops in an almost unstoppable force. France, Belgium, Holland, Poland, and the whole of the nations he spewed his wrath through, and suffered incredible hardships and were brutally pounded.

Although the long, first decade were characterized by a difficult financial associated situation as a result of the Great Depression, Deutsche Luft Hansa continued to expand its global network of courses in South America and dispatched booked flights of Germany towards in the Middle East. Strategically, the heads of the organization resulted in the rise of the Nazi Party; an airplane was made available for Adolf Hitler for his mission to run for president in the 1932 election, free of charge. Erhard Milch who was acting as the chief of the aviation company since 1926, was transformed into an authority on high-positioning at the Aviation Ministry when Hitler took the control of the ministry in 1933.

One of the main motivations for Deutsche Luft Hansa around then was the reduction of delivery times for mail. In 1930 in 1930, the Eurasia Corporation was established in a joint venture with Chinese automobile service granting Luft Hansa a syndication position to handle mail transportation between Germany and China and China, as well as admission for China. Chinese market. To this end, the Shanghai-Nanjing-Beijing course began in the next year utilizing Junkers W 34 sent there. Record-breaking times were established in the year 1930, when the mail route of Vienna to Istanbul (with trips to Budapest, Belgrade, and Sofia) ended in 24 hours. According to research, the primary journey by transoceanic airplane (from Warnemunde to New York City with an aircraft called the Dornier Wal) was a long time.

After many tests and testing, a scheduled postal route was created, in Europe as well as South America, in 1934. It was the most commonly booked administration of an ocean anywhere on the planet. The Wal aircraft were employed as slings dispatched for the overseas portion. These were carried by Dornier Do 18 in each of the 1936 creation events with the least visual conditions possible. The European organisation was able to see that the Junkers G.38 (around that time the largest traveler aircraft in the world) in the course Berlin-London using Amsterdam similar to it did the Junkers Ju 52/3m as well as the Heinkel He 70, which included faster flight times. Its innovations were backed by "Barrage services" (German: Blitzstrecken) between Berlin, Hamburg, Cologne and Frankfurt. By 1935, the first plane that was not manufactured in Germany entered the Luft Hansa armada: two Boeing 247s and a Douglas DC-2.

At the beginning of the conflict on September 1 1939, all citizen flights by Luft Hansa stopped, and the armada of aircrafts was put to the command from the Luftwaffe along with the majority of personnel. The Luftwaffe focused its efforts on the repair and support of aircrafts. Similar to the majority of German efforts in the conflict, it depended on limited work. They did their part and recruited its own employees who were confined to the workshops close to the frontline. There was no plan for traveler tours within Germany and non-involved nations, but appointments were restricted and fulfilled the demands of the war. In the final long durations during the war, the vast majority of travelers' aircrafts were converted to military vessels.

Luft Hansa's Luft Hansa co-activities in foreign nations were destroyed. Deruluft stopped was shut down after mediation by Chinese government. Syndicate Condor nationalized and renamed Cruzeiro do Sul in 1943 in an attempt to erase it of its German roots.

The last flight booked by Deutsche Luft Hansa - from Berlin to Munich took place on the 21st of April 1945, however, the plane went down in seconds prior to the scheduled appearance. A different (non-booked) trip was carried out the next day between Berlin to Warnemunde in the direction of the flight's activities. After the surrender of Germany and the subsequent Allied control over Germany the entire fleet of aircrafts within the country were confiscated, in addition, Deutsche Luft Hansa was dissolved. The remainder of the benefits were swapped on January 1st January, 1951.

On January 31, 1917 Germany declared the recharging of all submarine warfare throughout the Atlantic as German torpedo-equipped submarines are preparing to attack any boat that are regular citizens' transporters, which are supposed to be in combat zones.

In the year World War I started in 1914 The president Woodrow Wilson promised nonpartisanship for the United States, which most Americans believed in. However, England was one of America's closest trading partners and tensions soon erupted among and the United States and Germany over their attempt to blockade Britain. British Isles. Some U.S. ships heading out towards Britain were struck by German mines. Moreover in February

1915 Germany declared war on all vessels, neutral or not in the conflict zone in the vicinity of Britain. After a period of time, Germany reported that a German cruiser had destroyed the William P. Frye, an private American trader vessel that was transporting grain to England after it disappeared. President Wilson was furious, however, the German government was apologetic, considering the incident to be a grave error.

The Germans the most significant sea-based weapon was the U-vessel. which was a submersible that was unquestionably more sophisticated than the ones used by other nations at that time. for a long time the standard U-pontoon was at 214 feet, carried 35 soldiers as well as 12 torpedoes. They could be submerged for up to two hours continuously. In the early days during World War I, the U-vessels adversely affected the transportation of allies.

At the beginning the month of May, 1915 a handful of New York papers distributed an announcement from the German Embassy at Washington that Americans traveling aboard British or Allied vessels in conflict zones were doing so on their own responsibility. The announcement was made also an advertisement for the mandatory cruise of the British-owned Lusitania shipping liner between New York to Liverpool. On May 7th the Lusitania was torn down without warning completely off the banks of Ireland. Of the 1,959 passengers on board who were killed, 1,198 were killed which included 128 Americans.

On February 22nd, Congress approved the $250 million charge for arms appointments designed to help prepare to prepare the United States for war. In the course of two days British agents handed an U.S. envoy to Britain an exact copy of what has been called the "Zimmermann Note,"" the secret message of German Foreign Minister Arthur Zimmermann to Count Johann von Bernstorff who is who was the German ambassador to Mexico.

The message, which was captured as well as translated by British, Zimmermann expressed that should there be a conflict between Mexico and an adversary like the United States, Mexico ought to be invited to join the conflict as the German partner. In the end, Germany would vow to bring back Mexico the lost territory of Texas, New Mexico, and Arizona.

The history students at the clinical level have recently been able to access documents that prove that medical professionals were in reality in the hands of Nazis and became victims if they were identified as non-Aryan. Fangerau spoke about his findings together with Corinna Hartmann as well as Andreas Jahn of Gehirn & Geist Brain & Geist, the neuroscience and brain science journal of Spektrum der Wissenschaft, and the German counterpart of Scientific American.

A new report of the meeting follows.

The educator Fangerau is an exam venture examines the faked by experts of the nervous system during the Nazi time period. What is the reason this only a brief period following?

There were distinct phases in which individuals fought National Socialism following World War II. After 1945, the Allies pursued a plan of denazification. Then, German culture, in general, attempted to suppress its history. A lot of people from the generations to come believed it was hard to look away students in 1968 were angry that their leaders were not willing to take on their country's Third Reich. The strengths of the clinical system took longer to begin working to sort out the previous. Therefore, their review of the misconduct they had reported began in the 1980s.

One of the reasons why the recording of examinations into the nervous system has been conducted in a timely manner in recent years is because both psychiatry and the nervous system were joined into a common structure of disciplinary research in 1935. Prior to this, the research into the nervous system was beginning to separate from the field of psychiatry. The idea was to delegate mental wonders that are difficult to understand to experts and focus on issues which are self-evident in their anatomy. The National Socialists rejected the idea. They recognized that they could manage these strengths in the clinical field more successfully if they joined them with the Society of German Neurologists and Psychiatrists that was dominated by therapists who emphasized the notion of racial hygiene. The chief administrator of the population included Ernst Rudin, a therapist. So, the field of nervous system science has become less of a target. Since the end of the 1980s, a scientifically valid examination provides a completely different image.

Control of the nervous system was definitely at the forefront of the crimes committed by the Nazis. The concept of racial hygiene coupled with a sharp debate about the need for sympathy and cost reductions helped to justify the deliberate execution of more than 70,000 disabled people. The Nazis used the metaphor of killing. Two specialists in the nervous system and therapists were also included and it was often difficult to tell who is an expert in the nervous system and who was an expert. The experts surveyed patients and whoever they found to be dangerous or insufficient for the job was sent to an execution office and then killed. Neuroscientists at the time employed the cerebrums from deceased patients to conduct their investigations.

Hallervorden was the director of "auxiliary examination" to determine the purposeful elimination of the victims with illnesses as the highest of the histopathology department. Alongside other matters the team looked into which neurological and mental illnesses are passed down through the generations. These results shaped the rationale why patients were chosen to be killed. In the Kaiser Wilhelm Institute got vast numbers of cerebrums containing killing victims for its examination. In addition, as we are aware, those who participated in that test were aware of their origins.

Clinical experimentation that was not vetted (without tolerance assent or shields) conducted in the Third Reich is divided into three categories.

1. Tests to ensure the endurance of military personnel

A variety of trials are were planned to increase to improve the performance of Axis military officers on the field. For instance, in Dachau physicians who were part of The German flying corps as well as The German Experimental Institution for Aviation conducted high-elevation probes for detainees to select the highest distance at where groups of a damaged plane could parachute to safety. Researchers also conducted freezing probes on detainees in order to find a effective solution to hypothermia.

Detainees were also used to evaluate different ways of making the seawater drinkable.

2. Analyses to determine the effectiveness of medications and medications

Different studies have been developed and tested treatments and medications methods for injuries and illnesses that German army and occupation troops encountered on the battlefield. Researchers used prisoners from camps to test vaccine mixes and antibodies in anticipation of the cruel German prisons that were held at Sachsenhausen, Dachau, Natzweiler, Buchenwald, and Neuengamme. Prisoners were also employed to treat infectious diseases such as intestinal sickness tuberculosis, typhus, yellow fever, typhoid fever and irresistible hepatitis. Doctors from Ravensbruck conducted research on bone-joining, and also tried the recently developed Sulfa (sulfanilamide) medications. In Natzweiler and Sachsenhausen prisoners were exposed to mustard gas and phosgene to determine the effectiveness of possible treatments.

3. Analyses to help propel Nazi political and racial objectives:

The third category of clinical experimentation attempted to advance the racial as well as philosophical tenets of the Nazi viewpoint. The most famous was the work by Josef Mengele on twins of any age in Auschwitz. He also coordinated his investigations on Roma (Gypsies) like was Werner Fischer at Sachsenhausen, to determine how remarkable "races" were able to withstand various diseases. The study by August Hirt in Strasbourg University likewise proposed to establish "Jewish race mediocrity." Further grisly analysis to promote Nazi goals of racial equality included the process of Sanitization (View this Term on the Glossary) tests that were conducted in Auschwitz as well as Ravensbruck. Researchers attempted a variety of methods with the aim of create a successful and inexpensive method of massive cleaning.

The Nuremberg Code

Nuremberg Code Nuremberg Code was made in the aftermath of the disclosure of camp analyses and subsequent preliminary reports to address medical experts' recommendations throughout the Holocaust. It was the Nuremberg Code incorporated the guideline of educated assent and the required guidelines for research.

Chapter 7: The Treasure

From whispers in WWII to a brief description in the film Raiders of the Lost Ark There's always been speculation in the field of history about the existence of gold, art and other valuables which were taken during Nazis. Nazi regime. We'll take a closer look at "the largest robbery ever in the history of mankind" as per Guinness.

We do know that when Germans discovered and seized the Jewish people and sacked them of their possessions including gold jewellery, which they destroyed and engraved with the stamp from the German bank. They took advantage of every village they took over and kept any riches they could. They also robbed the reserves and banks of these nations, while keeping the currency. This led to a huge amount of the assets they utilized to support the war effort but the issue was. What is the best place to store this amount of valuable treasure? A treasure of this size can't be stored easily.

The first time, prior to the gold was made into bars , was stamped with their stamps from Reichsbank which was the German central bank a lot of the gold was held within the Reichsbank. This changed in 1945. in February, to be precise. The head of the German bank was the one who had the majority of its reserves shipped 200 miles from Berlin in the direction of Merkers. The town was home to an underground mine of potassium, where they kept art treasures from other countries and Germany.

Merkers was arrested in April 1945, by an Army regiment led by general Patton. There were French miners who revealed to the troops about the treasures hidden within the underground mine. A hoard of 8,198 gold bullion bar, silver bars, gold coins and paper money-all of which could be worth $520 million by 1945. This does not include the trove which was hiding in Berlin.

Due to the Allied forces that were advancing into Germany, Reichsbank called to transfer the remaining unjustly accumulated gains to Oberbeyern which is located situated in the southern part of Bavaria. It was here that the German forces believed they could stand their ground and regroup for a while. According to reports, nine tons of gold was delivered to the town along with currency and coins from foreign countries. After everything had been said and done troops from the U.S. troops were able to retrieve $11 million from the hoard and left $3 million in the air.

The Tracking of the Hoard

There is a legend about a woman that lived into the Austrian Alps. The name of her was Ida Weisenbacher. The Nazi army knocked at her front door and asked her to hook on a wagon that they loaded with boxes that were stamped with numbers and letters. Once the wagon was loaded, Ida was told to take the wagon to Lake Toplitz. When she reached the shore, soldiers already present would bring the boxes to drop them into the water and wait until they had completely submerged before taking another. It took three trips. Did this happen to be the location the location where the hoard that was missing was stored? Stern is a German magazine, would be able to be able to answer this question by examining the lake. They didn't find gold, but crates stuffed of counterfeit British pounds documents, secret documents as well as an printing press.

What Does This Mean?

What was discovered were the remains from Operation Bernhard. This was the brainchild of Hitler himself. He enlisted skilled engravers and printers from prison camps to create currency plates and make counterfeit currency. The goal was to fund the war effort and simultaneously throwing the economies of adversaries nations into a downward spiral. According to reports, an amount worth of $4.5 million dollars was forge and forged, with the majority comprised of British pounds. While they did also want to create

American currency but the war was over before any amount that would be considered to be significant was created.

The Austrian government in 1963, declared it illegal diving into Lake Toplitz after a German diver was killed trying to determine if more treasure was hiding in there. The government, determined to find out the truth of the matter, launched an underwater operation of their own and found additional crates of fake cash, mines, projectiles rockets and other experimental weapons. It is believed that the lake was used for the testing of torpedoes.

The lake was believed to be totally cleared in 1983, however Prof. Hans Fricke had been looking for evidence that life was present in this oxygen-deficient lake. The biologist discovered bacteria as well as the worm was alive under those conditions. He also found more counterfeit money as well as weapons for military use. He did not find any of the gold that was rumored to be fabled however, that didn't do much to dispel the notion of gold floating in the lake.

CBS together as well as The World Jewish Congress, sponsored an entire trip to investigate the lake with Oceaneering Technologies. Utilizing a remote-controlled sub, they were able to search every inch of the deepest part of Lake. The only thing they came across was British pounds.

A Cauldron has been discovered!

It's likely that after all the dives you've done with the itch for curiosity and thoughts of lost treasures had gone into the realm of legend However, in 2003, in the lake of Chiemsee in Bavaria the curiosity renewed. The reason is that an amateur diver discovered a cauldron that was made of solid gold and decorated by Celtic as well as Indo-Germanic scenes. It is believed that this cauldron came from an order piece from an Nazi official. It is 23 pounds, and its estimated value is just under $100,000.

The Secret Missions

There are also secret missions that are generally conducted in conflicts, skirmishes and wars. The Nazis did not differ in this respect, however their operations in secret has been an object of fascination and interest for a long time after the war. From the usual secret to the bizarre and the bizarre, it appears that the Nazis did everything from covert operations to secret missions, including failing to complete the rescue.

Hitler's Pirates

The nine ships appeared like peaceful cargo ships that are actually German trade raiders. They would fool other ships by waving non-neutral flags, or the flags of allies nations. Under the dark they would take over tanks and attack them, frequently helped by fog to cover themselves. It was the Royal Navy chased them for nearly three years, from one coast to the next. The pirates would take over or sink over a million tonnes of shipping goods.

They carried a dazzling collection of hidden weapons that were concealed by the structures or the crates for packing on deck. They would steal food and fuel. These ships would usually be in the sea for months, and sometimes for years. They would also transport goods into German U-boats.

It was the British Operation that Failed Badly

In a case that was deleted from German history There was a group comprised of German Special Forces that landed in the Isle of Wight. The Intel declared that it would be a straightforward operation and that the only obstacle was those of the Home Guard, elderly and disabled individuals who offered to guard England. When they arrived, it was not a pleasant reception. Highly skilled British commandos arrived to face German

Special Forces. German Special Forces, nearly taking them out completely. The thought was to steal items from St. Lawrence RAF radar station. The records were altered to show that there was no German forces ever touched the ground on British territory, except for those in the Channel Islands.

Mussolini's Daring Rescue

It was the year 1943 and Italy was on the verge of being defeated. Counselors of Mussolini tried to convince him to be a part of a deal with the Allies. Mussolini was adamant. On the 10th day of July, Allied troops arrived in Sicily which was welcomed by the Sicilians. The German troops were exiled by mid August, and they used their Strait of Messina to get to the mainland. Mussolini demanded assistance from Hitler However, The Battle of Stalingrad had destroyed the majority of the German forces. The Germans were not able to help Italy.

Mussolini requested an assembly with Mussolini called for a meeting of the Fascist Grand Council. The meeting lasted for 10 hours and many called for Mussolini to be removed. The dictator made an hour-long speech in which he pleaded with his fellow fascists to join forces to defeat the Allied forces, however, was not heeded by anyone in the gathering. The final vote of the council was 19-8 for Grandi's favour, which put the King Victor Emmanuel III in power. The next day, the king informed Mussolini that he was the most hated person throughout Italy as well as dismissed him with an apology. Mussolini was detained and put in jail. The new government was elected without fascists, and the populace was thrilled. Italy changed sides and was an integral part of Allied forces. The king, along with his government was forced to leave and leave the Northern part of Italy for the Germans.

Mussolini under house arrest was moved around constantly to avoid being discovered. This was the time it was transferred from the prison to Campo Imperatore, a Hotel in the mountains of Gran Sasso where the rescue was set to occur. The hotel was empty of guests, aside from the former leader who was treated as guests than prisoners. The Germans were able to locate him through using radio signals and coding communications.

The procedures for the rescue turned out to be a challenge. It was a ski area, located in the midst of the mountain making it difficult for the parachute to drop. It was airfield just behind the resort, however. Colonel. Otto Skorzeny decided that was the best location for landing a group of gliders. It wasn't until September 12, 1943, which was the date of the operation, that Col. Otto Skorzeny realized that the field wasn't flat, it was a steep hill. They were forced to fly over the entry point of the hotel. It was secured.

The carabinieri, also known as Italian security guards were wiped out without firing a shot. How? How? Italian General, Fernando Soleti, emerged from one of the gliders and yelled at guards to not shoot. In the chaos Skorzeny swung his gun at the radio operator before rushing up the steps. Mussolini was transported to a small Start and Landing plane in waiting. The commandos taken off by the foot.

The disappearing U-Boat

U-Boats, also known as submarines, were employed for different reasons during World War II, but they were not as popular as U-513. In the 10th of January, 1942, when it was officially launched the submarine was said to have been launched without official approval in late October or early November, the year before. The crew who claimed that it was in water when they were able to board her. She then left Hamburg to begin her journey six days later.

Her reputation was first established in the month of September 1942, waiting for a while in Conception Bay off Bell Island and spotting a 3,000-ton freighter. The freighter sailed into Wabana harbor, where U-513 fell 80 feet deep into the water and waited for a better location. A steamer that weighed 9,000 tons was spotted by the crew however, they were fortunate enough to encounter an adversary so eager to conduct the first test live they did not place the battery on torpedoes of Charge to Fire, causing the ordinance to sink into below the level of the harbour.

They were capable of sinking their target in the second shot. The watchers on the steamer did not see the submarine breach the surface prior to firing. The remainder of her first patrol also included sinking vessels within Bonavista Bay, St. Johns and followed an unidentified convoy was taken beyond its operational range.

The second patrol was not success. The unit was assigned to operate in the

Trinidad region. After seven days, oil filters inside diesel engines became blocked, as did the injectors. Impurities in the fuel were identified as the main cause of engine issues. The crew was instructed to wash the engine, and then run the test for 24 hours at high speed. Test results had to be presented to the Admiral after conclusion. The lever rods as well as the stems for valves are bent. U-513 returned to Lorient. Later, it was discovered that the paint on the aluminum had flaked off and had been absorbed to the engine. Due to the issues with the engines, the 3rd patrol was launched in the late afternoon. U-513 went on four patrols, and managed to add another to the ships that were sunk.

She was destined to die on the 19th of July 1943 to the south of Santos. It was able to spot and engage an aircraft that was heading towards it. The gunners began firing anti-aircraft weapons at the bomber in order to begin evasive maneuvers in order to avoid being struck from the blaster. During the war the U-513 fired both the 37mm as well as the 20mm anti-aircraft guns, but the second one stopped firing after a several rounds. The submarine was destroyed. There were seven survivors of the battle, however after the region was searched to locate it and the U-513 was not located. It wasn't found until nearly 68 years after the battle.

Chapter 8: Was Hitler Mad?

There are many theories regarding Hitler's health, and how he sought to conceal his illness from his fellow citizens. As the war progressed and his health declined, it appeared that he was sliding deeper into madness, but did this madness stem from mental issues or some other cause? In reality, Hitler had a myriad of health issues that tried to hide from his own people.

His physical health

In the last few years, most people are aware of Hitler being diagnosed with Parkinson's disease. It is possible to see the progress of the disease in news footage. The initial appearance is Adolf concealing one arm. This is because of the arm's tremors and later, in the reels, it is evident that you can see him moving around while walking. The issue with this theory lies in the physician he rely on, Doctor Morell, who was a snob in many circles, however, since his work "cured" the flatulence of Hitler the German leader was adamant about the doctor. Morell at one time was Hitler taking around 90 drugs. It was never really confirmed that Parkinson's disease existed.

Syphilis

It is believed that a lot of the symptoms Hitler showed in later reels were due to Syphilis at late stages. This means he was suffering from the illness for many years. The symptoms mentioned above aswell being a heartbeat that was irregular. There are many historians who claim that he was obsessed by the disease because of the fact that he devoted 14 pages to Mein Kampf and even self diagnosed himself to a certain point. The author was also famous for calling it an "Jewish condition". In his book, he outlined his desire to be a prostitute as well as the spread in the spread of this disease. While it's not been confirmed, historians believe this is the reason for Hitler's tendency to stay clear of normal sexual relationships. If you are trying to find images of Hitler showing off his torso you're not likely to find anything.

There aren't any known photos of his body or wearing the bathing suit.

The Drug Addiction

If you've seen documentaries, you've likely been aware of his habit of taking drugs. Morell as we mentioned earlier was Hitler taking over 90 prescriptions. The list includes injections. The average dose was 3 injections, 120 pills per daily. The most common drugs were methamphetamine, barbituratesand opiates as well as cocaine.

Mental Problems

Many believe that Hitler suffered from mental illness However, none of these claims has been proved. It's possible to speculate that, given the type and quantity of medication he consumed his mind was in a haze of drugs. It could have contributed to his uncontrollable behavior, his irrational orders to fight and perhaps even anxiety to a certain degree.

CPSIA information can be obtained
at www.ICGtesting.com
Printed in the USA
LVHW080000061222
734629LV00016B/1175

9 781998 769223